Ghosts
of San Francisco

Kathryn Vercillo

4880 Lower Valley Road   Atglen, Pennsylvania   19310

Dedication

This book is dedicated to everyone in my life who asks with genuine interest about what I'm doing, and then doesn't blink an eye when I say that I'm writing a book about San Francisco's ghosts. It is especially dedicated to my family (and to friends both old and new) who have given me the support that I need to realize all of the crazy dreams that get in to my head. I hope that the afterlife truly is real so that I can continue to enjoy knowing you long after we have left this world.

Published by Schiffer Publishing Ltd.
4880 Lower Valley Road
Atglen, PA 19310
Phone: (610) 593-1777; Fax: (610) 593-2002
E-mail: Info@schifferbooks.com

For the largest selection of fine reference books on this and related subjects, please visit our web site at
www.schifferboooks.com.
We are always looking for people to write books on new and related subjects. If you have an idea for a book please contact us at the above address.

This book may be purchased from the publisher.
Include $3.95 for shipping.
Please try your bookstore first.
You may write for a free catalog.

In Europe, Schiffer books are distributed by
Bushwood Books
6 Marksbury Ave.
Kew Gardens
Surrey TW9 4JF England
Phone: 44 (0) 20 8392-8585; Fax: 44 (0) 20 8392-9876
E-mail: info@bushwoodbooks.co.uk
Website: www.bushwoodbooks.co.uk
Free postage in the U.K., Europe; air mail at cost.

Copyright © 2007 by Kathryn Vercillo
Library of Congress Control Number: 2007925255

Designed by Mark David Bowyer
Type set in Burton's Nightmare 2000 / New Baskerville BT

ISBN: 978-0-7643-2765-0
Printed in China

Contents

Introduction

Ghosts, spirits, the living dead ... any number of different names and descriptions can be applied to those shadowy characters which linger in the corners of our waking lives, watching over us while working out their own histories. No matter what name they are given, interest in these beings has been a part of nearly every culture throughout all of time. And San Francisco is a city where different cultural traditions can blend together to allow a large number of people to gain exposure to different beliefs about the afterlife, a city where an open-minded attitude allows people to suspend their own doubts and disbelief and simply let themselves see what might be out there at all levels of life and death.

More than almost anywhere else in the world, San Francisco is a city in which cultures merge, and the oral traditions of one generation are related to the next through those cultures to create a fabric woven of shared histories, a fabric which transcends the distinct cultures of its origination. The historical beliefs of a given culture in what may happen in the afterlife come together with modern new age mythology and scientific findings to create a city which is filled with an almost awe-inspiring acceptance that there are many different methods of viewing the world around us. Through this openness, San Francisco has become a city which is filled with different versions of the same ghost stories along with new ghost stories cropping up on a regular basis.

The ghosts which are said to haunt this city are as diverse and interesting as the people who populate San Francisco's geographic borders today. Whether or not you personally believe in the ghost world, what you will find when exploring the tales of ghosts in San Francisco is that the stories told here are part of the history of the city; through learning these stories, you will learn intimate details about San Francisco's past. Understanding the past is crucial to understanding the present and moving in to the future; an exploration of the reported ghosts of the area improves the well-rounded collection of such understanding.

Unfortunately, one of the greatest causes for spirits to linger in the waking world is a restlessness associated with an untimely death. San Francisco has been home to a number of tragedies over the years, which is one of the reasons why it may be a location favored by spirits. The 1906 earthquake is one of the greatest tragedies of the area. In addition to the collapsing of numerous buildings throughout the area, the earthquake caused fires which devastated the city, resulting in a number of crushing deaths. It was less than a century later that another earthquake (Loma Prieta) hit the area. Although the death count of the 1989 quake was low, its effect was undeniably unsettling, and the people of the Bay Area all share a history which includes these effects.

Sometimes the tragedies which cause spirits to linger are singular events. Suicides and murders fall into this category. However, in San Francisco, these experiences are often linked to a greater collective history than may be true of other areas. This is because of the tendency for a large number of people to experience similar events in the city resulting from the constant influx of new faces in to the San Francisco scene. The Golden Gate Bridge is known worldwide as a spot for suicides, so much so that there are suicide hotline phones on either end of the famous landmark. To a lesser degree, the Bay Bridge has been a location where suicides have taken place. Because of the number of people taking their own lives in a single area, these areas have become wrought with emotional overtones, creating the setting for there to be ghosts hovering in the region.

There are also numerous historical tragedies in San Francisco which affected certain minority groups and made up the fabric of their history of life in the city. Chinese immigrants who traveled to the area through illegal means often suffered at the hands of a cruel human fate. Entire populations of people, including Native American groups and Jewish American groups, who once peacefully rested in their burial spots, were unearthed to make room for new buildings and new homes. San Francisco is a city which is built upon the bones of the past.

However, not all spirits lingering in San Francisco are here because they are stuck in a horrible time beyond which they can not seem to move. San Francisco is a vibrant city where life is lived to the fullest, and it seems that there are some spirits who stay here not because they can't move on, but merely because they do not want to leave the area. Often, these are travelers who were not from San Francisco originally, but who made it their second home; frequently these were celebrities in the social and literary worlds which pulsated in San Francisco during certain eras in the city's history. These ghosts returned to the area after their passing, not in order to resolve the past, but rather to re-live it; their years spent here were so glorious that they simply can not think of any better place to spend out their days.

San Francisco is an open and accepting place, and perhaps that is also part of the reason why the history of hauntings in this area is so closely linked with the history of the city itself. Perhaps a higher proportion of people living in the Bay Area are willing to suspend their cynicism about the spirit world and simply accept that there just may be many more levels to life and death than might appear at first glance. Or perhaps the vibrancy and constant change of the city leave doors open that let characters of life move easily between dimensions of this world.

When I began working on this book, my own beliefs in the spirit world were probably akin to the religious belief of agnosticism. My basic philosophy on life in general is that there are many factors working around and about us each day that we can neither see nor know. People are thinking of us, cultural trends are taking place, and perhaps spirits are watching over us. More or less, because I had no first-hand experience of ghosts, I just figured that it was something which I didn't know enough about to have formed an educated opinion about the topic.

However, as I started to research this book, and I began to tell people in my life what I was working on, what I discovered was that nearly everyone I knew or newly met had some sort of ghost story that they wanted to share. Given a willing audience of one with whom they felt comfortable, everyone from my personal trainer to the guy I'd just started dating came out with stories of their San Francisco homes and businesses which had once been haunted. They revealed their own lack of understanding about the topic as well as their own interest in learning more about the possibilities which might exist outside of the world which we take for granted on a regular basis.

For those people who believe wholly in the spirit world, I hope that this book offers an informative look at the spirits which have lingered throughout this fabulous city over time. And for those people who are less than inclined to believe in spirits as factual parts of history, I hope that this book can still be used to explore the true history of San Francisco, a history made up of unique individual experiences which merged together over time to create a shared story. We are the amalgamation of our experiences, and what came before us should be treasured for the ways in which it helped to create us and to bring us to where we are today. The world is a highly interconnected place and the stories of those around us—both living and dead—are a part of the collective story which helps to define who each of us is.

About This Book:
A Brief Guide to What's Inside

This book is designed for people with all different levels of interest in the ghost history of San Francisco, from the amateur ghost hunter who is interested in exploring the city's spirits on his (or her) own to the San Francisco traveler who would like to get an interesting perspective on the history of the city through the eyes of the characters who once populated the area. There is a little bit of something in this book for everyone with an interest in the city, and it is designed in such a manner so that readers can take from it what they will to enhance their knowledge of the area and their experience spending time in the city.

The book has seven different sections. The first five sections tell the stories of the different ghosts which have been reported to spend their time in San Francisco. Culled together from a combination of resources, including historical accounts, first person narratives and the folklore of various cultural segments of the city, these sections make up the bulk of the purpose of the book. They comprise the storytelling which is intended to be informational in terms of both the ghost history and the general history of the city of San Francisco.

These first five sections of the book organize the material in such a manner so that the reader can choose which types of haunted locations interest him or her the most. Although the book can be read straight through in its entirety to give a good overall picture of the history of the area and the ghosts who linger here, it can also be read helter skelter to meet the diverse interests of all of the readers who have an interest in the topic.

Perhaps you, as a reader, have a keen interest in the architectural history of San Francisco. If this is the case, the first section, which tells the stories of the hauntings of various homes and mansions within the city is probably the section for you—it will provide not only information about the characters who lived in San Francisco's homes, but also information about the types of homes built in the area at different times throughout history. Likewise, if the portion of San Francisco's past which interests you most is that of the number of famous people who have dwelt within the streets here, you may find that the section on haunted hotels, where those people spent their days and nights, is the section which reveals the most to you about those city personalities who have kept you entertained—even after their passing.

The last two sections of the book are designed less for the historical reader and more for the amateur ghost hunter. However, they may be of interest to the average reader for the additional information that they convey about the city. Part VI reveals the biographical and professional information of a number of experts who have contributed to the ghost stories of San Francisco in recent times. These include well-known psychics and lesser-known local mediums who are spending their lives connecting with the dead. Part VII offers information to the new ghost hunter, about how to go about designing a ghost hunt of his (or her) own.

I encourage you to jump around as much or as little as you would like to get the most that you can out of the material which lies before you. For those people who have come to accept the possibility that there may be spirits among us, there is the sense that life is not lived in any sort of linear fashion despite our greatest attempts to tell our stories as though it is. In the spirit of opening ourselves up to the idea that there is a sort of timelessness and this lack of linear progression, feel free to simply open up the book and let the stories find you.

Hopefully, in the end, you will find that reading this book has allowed you the opportunity to do some adventuring of your own. Challenge your own assumptions. Let history unfold in front of you as though it could be happening around you today. And if you decide that you truly want to live a life which might brush up against the unexpected, the last section of the book—with its tips for how to hunt San Francisco's ghosts down for yourself—may prove to be more useful than you thought at the start of your reading.

Part I:
Homes / Mansions

When tragedy occurs in a particular location, spirits may feel the need to linger in that location. Perhaps they have unresolved business there that they wish to take care of before they move on. Or perhaps they simply do not like it when they feel that others are encroaching on what they still consider to be their personal space. Whatever the case may be, there are many instances in which a spirit is associated with a particular home or building, haunting one new resident after another until whatever it was that was bothering that particular spirit is located and resolved.

One of the types of locations most frequently found to be haunted in San Francisco is the personal homes and old mansions which have been lived in by various people throughout the years. More so than office buildings, places of worship, and famous landmarks, the homes of a city are where the heart tends to remain. In death, people may find that they want to get back to where their hearts were last felt beating. San Francisco is a very transient location. People move in and out easily and frequently over time—and sometimes those who are moving in discover that the others haven't quite yet moved out.

For San Franciscans, home is intricately linked with history. Being a small city in geographic terms, development has been more upward than outward, with large buildings growing ever-larger as construction capabilities improve. Homes have stories within their walls which transcend the time that the residents usually know about. The home can be one of the most unsettling places for the living to experience the dead. The home is meant to be a safe haven, a sanctuary from the rest of the world. When the safety of the home is taken away, individuals find themselves feeling lost. For this reason, it is most frequently personal homes to which exorcists and mediums are called to find out what is happening in the spirit world. Home is the one place where people do not want the undead to spend their time.

And yet, they do.

Post Street Home:
The Mystery of a Haunted House

What determines the location which a ghost might haunt? In general, it is the site where a tragedy occurs. In some cases, it is the favorite location of a deceased person who wants to return to happier times. In other cases, the spirit seems to be following the movements of a loved one in the hopes of sending them a message or just in the interest of watching out for them. In the case of the Post Street Home, it is difficult to say what the motivation might be for the spirits who stuck around within its walls because the home itself has been moved multiple times.

This fact reveals an interesting part of San Francisco history. Today, of course, when we buy a home, we also buy the property on which that home is built. The two purchases almost always go hand-in-hand. However, in the late nineteenth century, this was not how such things were done. At that time, a home and the property upon which one might live were purchased separately, and the home would be de-constructed and reconstructed on the new property. In effect, you would purchase the lot or location on which you would like to live, and then you would separately purchase the home which you found most suitable to your preference, and then you would merge the two by moving the old building to the new site. It was almost similar in fashion to the concept of the mobile home in modern times, although the process was one which required considerably more effort, considering the fact that the homes were generally designed to last in one location for a long period of time.

Such was the case with the home which was once located at 924 Post Street, near the intersection of Post and Larkin in what is known today as the Tenderloin neighborhood. Originally, the Post Street home was located several blocks down from the address at 924 Post Street, although it became known as The Post Street Home because it was on Post Street even in its original location (Richards, 2004, p. 27). Upon first being built at this original location (in the middle of the nineteenth century), the exterior of the Post Street Home was constructed and of course plans were made to complete the internal design (Richards, 2004, p. 25). However, the owner of the home ran out of money and the interior was never built. In an interest-ing architectural twist, the home didn't even have a door—entrance to the building was gained through an underground passageway which decomposed after a time, leaving the exterior shell of a house without any way to access the inside.

Well, at least no way for the living.

From the time that it was first built back in the 1860's, the Post Street Home was reported to be haunted. Neighbors of the area would gather outside to see if activity was taking place, as this was big news in what was a small city at the time. And news it was, because it was presented in quite a factual manner, during a time when most people believed in ghosts without question. The story of the haunted house made headlines when it was happening and it re-appeared in the *San Francisco Examiner* in 1893, approximately thirty years after the house had been built but not lived in (Richards, 2004, p. 26).

There were several different ghosts reported as sighted at the original Post Street location of the home. The gray-haired ghost of an elderly woman would appear in an upstairs window—a location where it would be impossible for a living woman to be since there was no interior floor built which could reach the area (Richards, 2004, p. 28). Her apparition would hover there in the window, looking down at the onlookers who were looking back at her in astonishment as they tried to figure out who she was and how she had managed to find her way into the home. She made only slight movements and never gave any indication as to what it was that she was seeking from her position inside of the half-built home. She bothered no one intentionally, but many in the neighborhood felt bothered by even the idea that she was present there among them. Although acceptance of spirit activity was more widespread among the general population at the time that she was seen, scientific advancements were making it less acceptable to those in the area to consider that she might be a ghost. And yet, there was no other explanation for how this elderly woman, who only appeared occasionally and who never seemed to change in appearance, could possibly be looking out from the second story of a home which had no staircase.

In addition to this woman, the spirit of a man apparently spent time in the home because the screams of an adult male would be heard by passersby (Richards, 2004, p. 28). For a period of several months, it seemed that these two spirits—or perhaps others who had also found a way in to the doorless home—were deeply engaged in a heated debate. The clattering of ongoing arguments was recognized around the neighborhood as originating from that home; and yet when the home was finally accessed, there was no sign of any sort of debris or damage at all (Richards, 2004, p. 28). Whatever had been slamming and cracking and slapping on all of those nights when the neighbors gathered to determine the source of the sound was apparently something which did not leave any sort of mark behind. The neighbors were never able to explain the happenings of the home.

The activity continued during the entire lifetime of the home as it was at that location. Eventually, a new buyer became interested in the house despite the history of spirit activity associated with the location. Perhaps he was a disbeliever in the presence of ghosts. Or perhaps he thought that the ghosts were likely to be attached to the physical property on which the home was built, and that by moving the home he could avoid having to deal with the spirits. Indeed, he purchased the building and moved it to the location at 924 Post Street which is the location in which it spent the longest amount of time, and the location which turned out to be the one which was best known in the area by those interested in spirit activity (Richards, 2004, p. 27).

Although the new owner originally planned to live in the home, his interest waned when the hauntings continued despite the physical move of the building to the new property. In fact, the activity was so intense from the very beginning of the owner's purchase of the home, that he never built the inside of the house at all. He left the building to near-total abandonment, a decision which only increased the activity there. Although sounds and sightings were regularly reported at this time, there is no known record of who the ghosts might be that were apparently present in the home. It is only known that many of the people who lived in the area surrounding the unfinished house felt a sense of eerie discomfort during the time that the home was there because of the significantly large amount of ghost activity which was taking place within the walls of the unfinished building (Richards, 2004, p. 28).

The haunted home was later purchased by a man by the name of Mr. Campbell who moved the building once again, this time to Fulton and Divisadero (Richards, 2004, p. 29). Perhaps the move of the building unsettled the spirits enough to move them out of the house, or perhaps when Mr. Campbell finished the interior of the building the ghosts got bored with their play space, because they seem to have neither followed the home nor remained in either of the original locations of the building on Post Street. No reports were made about those same spirits at any time after the building was moved by Mr. Campbell.

It is impossible, of course, to say what motivates a spirit to show up in any particular place. History usually indicates the identity of the spirit and points to some clues from which the living can infer; but the case of the Post Street Home is truly the Mystery of a Haunted House.

Atherton Mansion:
A Son and Husband's Revenge

The nineteenth century is filled with stories of rugged frontiersmen who moved west in search of not only riches, but also of adventure. The times were exciting and there was a buzzing energy in the air all around. Everyone wanted to develop their own new lives within this period of intense change. Men from all up and down the east coast pushed the edges of their own boundaries as they moved out in development of the area. And women pushed the edges of their own boundaries by moving with them and defining new ways for making a life.

Faxon D. Atherton was one of those men who felt that the boundaries of his own world should be limitless. Born in Massachusetts, he felt that urge to get out into the world to see what else was out there from the time that he was a young child (Haunted Bay, 2006). As soon as he got the opportunity, he took off in pursuit of what was then the American Dream (although it would actually take him a little while to return to America because he took a rather circuitous route to get there). While many of his fellow frontiersmen were making their way west, Atherton traveled south, heading all the way to Valparaiso, Chile where he became an established tradesman (Haunted Bay, 2006). A man who refused all limitations, he traded not only hides and furs but also food and any other goods he could get his hands on. This independent spirit was a businessman at heart, and his trade business thrived.

In the course of his career, he finally did move to the West Coast, taking Dominga de Goni with him as his bride (Haunted Bay, 2006). She was the daughter of a wealthy family, a woman known for her striking appearance and outstanding charm. Like many good girls, she was interested in the bad-boy pioneering spirit of Faxon D. Atherton. They moved to the Bay Area in 1860, and although the major gold rush was already over, Atherton had no trouble fitting his career into San Francisco life. Rapidly, he became known as one of the richest men in the area, making real estate purchases all up and down the California coast line and settling with his family in one of these locations just outside of the city of San Francisco (Haunted Bay, 2006). In fact, the town of Atherton, California is named after him, although this was done after his death and so is a fact to which he was never privy (Merriman, 2005).

Together, Atherton and his Chilean bride had seven children which they raised in their Bay Area home. However, domestic life failed to calm Atherton's frontiersmen attitude. Known in the area for his womanizing tendencies and his affection for extra-marital affairs, Atherton could not bring himself to stay chained to the small realm of his family home (Haunted Bay, 2006). He traveled often in order to escape the confines of his domestic life.

Atherton's travels left his wife alone in their home much of the time. In order to efficiently run a household of seven children without the domineering hand of a father figure strongly in place, Dominga de Goni had to become a powerful woman in her own right. Though she could not control her husband's philandering, she could take control of the situation in her own home and she did just that, ruling her large family with an iron fist (Haunted Bay, 2006).

Sometimes, Dominga's combined sense of helplessness in relation to her husband and sense of power in relation to her children caused her to spin out of control. Most often, her son George was the subject of her bouts of cruelty (Haunted Bay, 2006). Though he escaped in to a fantasy world in which he emulated his father's intense pursuits into the world around him, George remained physically at home with his mother.

When Faxon D. Atherton passed away, Dominga decided to leave the home that they had lived in together in order to move into the heart of the city. Using the resources culled from the melding of her wealthy family and her husband's career in trade, she had built for her a home which came to be known as the Atherton Mansion. Located at the intersection of Octavia and California Streets, at the address of 1990 California Street, the Atherton Mansion was one of the most exquisite homes of the then-highly-exclusive Pacific Heights neighborhood (Haunted Bay, 2006).

Living in the mansion with her was George who had failed to escape the restrictions of his mother's domineering presence. In fact, he had managed to double the trouble he had in his home by marrying a woman, Gertrude Franklin Horn, who was strikingly similar to his mother (Haunted Bay, 2006). Perhaps George had a mother complex of sorts, because he met the young Gertrude after a failed stint as the suitor of her mother (Merriman, 2005).

Gertrude was a writer who had failed to make a career for herself as an author, in part because her attitude was not conducive to creating the human connections necessary to thrive in the arts scene. Although she wrote extensively throughout her lifetime in the Bay Area and was published on a number of occasions, she failed to network in the manner necessary to establish herself as a writer at the time. This was enhanced by her coverage of certain controversial topics (Merriman, 2005). A stifled artist, she seemed to work hard to stifle those around her into experiencing the same kind of misery which she felt seemed to be her fate.

Indeed her attitude made it almost impossible for other authors to like her. She often failed to even meet people who could be essential to her career because she was so self-absorbed and demanding that she would opt to miss out on opportunities to save herself time or energy. For example, she opted not to meet Oscar Wilde when an introduction offer was made to her by a mutual friend because she thought that he was an unattractive man and she did not want to be seen or even be in the presence of someone she found so physically repugnant (Albert, 2006).

Even those people with whom Gertrude did become friends quickly found that her controlling and backstabbing ways made it difficult to enjoy her company. For example, she was friends with writer Ambrose Bierce until a time when he attempted to kiss her and, rather than evading the attempt quietly or dealing with it head on, she spent considerable time making fun of the situation amongst their friends until he no longer spent time with her (Albert, 2006). She also had problems with female authors due to an uncontrollable jealousy lingering in her heart for any success which they might have achieved which had eluded her. When Edith Wharton began gaining attention for her writing, Gertrude was quick to spread the rumor that Wharton had not been writing her own work, trying to stir up trouble in the literary world, but ultimately only creating discomfort for herself in that society (Albert, 2006).

Despite her difficulties in the writing field, Gertrude pursued her career wholeheartedly. In fact, she pursued this career almost single-mindedly, to the degree that some would say her career helped to make her home life unbearable for those around her. For example, she and George had a daughter, but the daughter was sent to live with relatives so that Gertrude could spend her time writing (Merriman, 2005). They also had a son but the son died at the tender young age of just six years old and Gertrude opted not to have other children after his death because she wanted to devote herself to creative pursuits (Merriman, 2005). There is nothing inherently wrong in Gertrude's decision, and perhaps it is to her credit that she knew herself well enough to buck the conventions of motherhood which were expected of her at the time. However, it does speak to the fact that it was her career which interested Gertrude first and foremost. Her failure to make a name for herself through that career led to increasing levels of creative frustration which she took out on those around her through violent outbursts, catty inclinations, and attempts at domination of the spirits of others.

A prolific writer, Gertrude completed more than forty novels. These novels speak to the heart of the situation in the Atherton home. The main character in nearly every single one of Gertrude's novels is a fiercely independent woman who controls the world around her in one way or another. This was the woman that Gertrude wanted to be at all times, although she didn't always succeed.

Gertrude may not have entirely controlled her own world, but she did her best to control her husband. She and George moved into the Atherton Mansion and the two ladies of the home—Dominga and Gertrude—seemed to almost compete as to which could do a better job of completely controlling every move that George made. They humiliated him in public and dominated him in private. They told him what to do, demeaned him for not doing it quite well enough, and encouraged each other in their mistreatment of him (Hauck, 2006).

In response, George withdrew even further into his own imagination. In his fantasies, George stood up to his wife and mother, emulating his father's strength and developing his own adventuresome life. In these fantasies, he would take a stand for himself, sometimes merely escaping the troubling twosome of his home and other times turning the tables on them and forcing them each to experience the same sort of harrowing humiliation which was regularly forced upon him in his real life. Most often, George escaped only temporarily, to drink with friends at a nearby tavern before returning home to the control of the women. In 1887, in a decision made while drinking with those friends, George decided to try to live out his fantasies of freedom (Haunted Bay, 2006). He escaped the finger-nailed clutches of the dominant women in his life under the pretense of going to Chile to visit some friends. Although the women were not happy about his plan, his small attempt at taking charge of his own life had a temporary effect which allowed him to get a small grip on his own fate. In his mind, the plan was to take after his father in setting up a life for himself thousands of miles away from his original home. He didn't have a set agenda for his arrival in Chile, but he certainly did not plan on returning home to the women of his life at any time in his foreseeable future (Hauck, 2006). George was out to make a new life for himself!

But alas, George simply lacked the frontiersmen attitude which had propelled his father into worldly success. George was just a little bit too much of his mother's son. He simply did not have the spirit in him that he needed to make the kind of move that he was trying to make when he spontaneously decided to take life by the horns and head out into adventure. He hadn't even reached Chile when he fell quite ill. His kidneys failed him and George died on the ship (Haunted Bay, 2006).

At the end of the nineteenth century, there was no option of turning the ship back and allowing for a proper burial of George Atherton. Doing the best that he could to help George in maintaining some sort of dignity in his death, the captain of the ship ordered that George's body be stored in a barrel of rum which would preserve it well enough to get it sent back home where the women of his life could do with George what they would, seemingly ending his life in the same way in which it had always been lived out, under the control of the Atherton women (Haunted Bay, 2006).

However, in death, George may have found the will to live his way. The barrel containing his body returned to the Atherton Mansion without any description indicating the contents held within. The butler opened the barrel in an attempt to obtain rum for a family party, finding instead George's rum-soaked body. The women of the home were disturbed to the point of becoming emotionally distraught, and it seemed to onlookers at the time that it may have been more than just the fact that their party was ruined that bothered them. Both women went pale-faced as soon as they saw the body and they never really acted the same after that. Although the body was dried out and given a proper burial, George seems to have refused to leave the Atherton Mansion (Haunted Bay, 2006).

Shortly after his death, both of the women in the home began to have problems with his spirit. They would hear knocking on their bedroom doors, only to get up and find that there was no one there. Frequently, they each felt that they were being watched by a cold, unsettling presence. They were uncomfortable in the Atherton Mansion at nearly every moment following the discovery of the body. Eventually, the women could bear these problems no longer. They sold the mansion and moved elsewhere, living out the rest of their lives separately, trying to get as far away from both the memory and the ghost of George Atherton as was physically possible.

Gertrude traveled throughout the world for a number of years, getting herself away from the San Francisco home and the fate that her writing and her personal life had found there. She spent time living in New York, Paris, and Germany, writing under both her own name and a number of pseudonyms. She eventually found that the pull of San Francisco was simply too great to leave it behind completely, and she returned to the city towards the end of her life. She finished out her days there and died within its boundaries in 1948, after which her cremated remains were placed at the Cypress Lawn Memorial Park Columbarium in nearby Colma (Merriman, 2005).

While Gertrude was busy living her life all over the world, George was apparently making a home for himself in the mansion that he had originally felt so emotionally stifled in. Perhaps George was pleased to have finally taken control of the situation in the Atherton Mansion, because he did not follow the women when they left, but instead appears to have stayed in the home. Maybe he liked the opportunity to finally have a chance to simply live comfortably in his home, taking control when he felt that it was necessary in order to assert himself in that way in which he had not learned to do during his relatively brief lifetime.

His knocking and the presence of cold spots throughout the home continued after the women moved. Despite the monetary value of the Atherton Mansion and its prime location within San Francisco's Pacific Heights neighborhood, tenants moved out of the home almost as quickly as they moved in, made uncomfortable by the haunting presence of George Atherton. Home owners wondered if anyone would ever again settle comfortably into life in the home.

But perhaps it just took another domineering woman to set George in his place, because in 1923 the mansion was purchased by a woman named Carrie Rousseau who managed not to be driven out by the odd occurrences (Haunted Bay, 2006). She lived in the home until her death in 1974. However, she lived only in the ball room of the house which was taken over by her collection of at least fifty cats and the occasional odd assortment of boarders (Haunted Bay, 2006). Maybe Rousseau was just the kind of woman who could co-exist with George Atherton's spirit. She was independent enough to be a woman he was familiar enough to relate to, but eccentric enough that she didn't have to challenge him for space. She never reported seeing his spirit in the home, but then she never really reported much of anything due to her solitary nature. Very little is known about the life of Carrie Rousseau, and, of course, this mystery creates much room for speculation by those who are interested in knowing about those things which can not quite be known.

Upon Rousseau's death, the Atherton Mansion was renovated and turned into apartments. Whether or not George had stayed quiet for all of those years or simply couldn't be heard above the mewing, his presence returned after Rousseau's death. Tenants in the renovated building have heard his knocking and felt the cold spots throughout the old home (Haunted Bay, 2006). Some have reported gusts of wind passing through rooms which are not exposed to open windows and others have reported hearing arguing voices (Haunted Bay, 2006).

No one could say for sure that it was George Atherton who was in the home at this time, but there was definitely a spirit in the building bothering those who lived there in modern times. Various reports would come through different channels as the people of the building tried to figure out what was going on in the home. Some accepted that George's spirit just might be continuing to try to assert some control over the changing situation in the building. Others weren't so sure.

The presence of ghosts was so troublesome that the experts were called in to help confirm the nature of the activity in the home. Sylvia Brown and Antoinette May (psychics/mediums known for their individual and joint-effort work in the Bay Area) combined efforts in a séance to reveal the source of the hauntings (Hauck, 2006). As a result of the findings of this séance, along with the detailed reports of those who have experienced the spirits for themselves, it is believed that there are now four ghosts lingering in the Atherton Mansion. George continues to try to stand up for himself against his wife and mother who have now made their way back to the mansion to deal in death with those details they could not settle in life (Haunted Bay, 2006). Gertrude Horn may have traveled far away when George first began his haunting of the home, but she returned to San Francisco at the end of her lifetime, and so it is really of no surprise that perhaps her spirit is still trying to work out the issues of its history within the walls of the Atherton Mansion where so many troubled nights were spent. While the Atherton family deals with its own past, it appears that Carrie Rousseau lingers on, making the home quite uncomfortable for the people who are trying to start new lives in this part of San Francisco today.

Donaldina Cameron House:
A Tragic Cultural Experience

The history of Chinese immigration to San Francisco is long and rich and involves many inspiring, as well as many devastating, stories of trouble and triumph over oppressive conditions. Perhaps most difficult to hear about are the histories of young Chinese girls who immigrated to the area at the end of the nineteenth and the beginning of the twentieth centuries.

At that time, only Chinese men were allowed relatively easy immigration into the United States, coming across the Pacific to make their livings working long hours in harsh conditions so that they could send money to their families back at home. Immigration of anyone other than single men was nearly impossible due to the passage of a series of three Chinese exclusion acts which started in 1882 (Thomas, 2003). Many of those single men who were coming over to the San Francisco area to make their new lives missed their families, and the chasm between that longing for their community and the legalities of bringing their families to the United States created a thriving illegal immigration route. The desire by Chinese men to bring Chinese women to the area through this route was enhanced by the fact that the series of Congressional acts also forbade the men from marrying non-Chinese women in the United States (Thomas, 2003). As a result, women were brought across the seas through various illegal channels, generally suffering under harsh conditions (Thomas, 2003).

Men from the upper classes were more easily able to get government approval to bring their families over from China than were men from lower classes (Thomas, 2003). Because of this, they would seek payment from lower class men in exchange for pretending to be related to the family of the lower class man to ease the process of immigration. Men from the lower classes would pay large sums of money for forged documents demonstrating a link between their family and one of these upper class men (Thomas, 2003). Sometimes, this worked. The men would pay the fee, their families would be sent over and they would live the rest of their lives together in relative peace. It was basically a simple business transaction.

But human history is filled with exploitation, and this sector of it is no exception. Many times, the process did not go as relatively smoothly as it did for those women who came over in business-like fashion. Instead, when the women of the family would arrive, the upper class men would hold them hostage, demanding even more payment from the men who had fought so hard to bring them over to the United States. The women, living in the country illegally, had no recourse (Thomas, 2003). Often, when the families failed to pay the increased fees, the women were sold into slavery. In fact, in addition to the illegal immigration of women trying to come to the area to meet their families, there was established a strong tradition of kidnapping women from China (primarily the Canton area) specifically to be sold into slavery in San Francisco (Thomas, 2003). The younger girls would be sold as house servants, a task which they would perform throughout their young adolescence, working for families all throughout the Bay Area. As these girls got older, they would join the older women in their families who had been sold into sex slavery. Illegal prostitution was common at this time due in part to the staggering difference in numbers of Chinese men compared to Chinese women in the area (Thomas, 2003).

With no legal reason for being in the United States and with only a limited understanding of both the laws and the language in San Francisco, the life of the sex slave was an unspeakable one. Abuse of all kinds was the norm and the life span of these women was short. And for the most part, this was a large-scale problem which went unnoticed or ignored by the larger Bay Area community. This was not an era when help for these women was easy to find.

However, there were a few angels working to make changes in the situation. One of these angels was Donaldina Cameron. Originally from New Zealand, she lived in the San Francisco area throughout her entire life (Thomas, 2003). She was an enterprising woman with a heart of gold and a desire to use her resources to help others. Before she was thirty, she had begun a lifelong pursuit of social justice in the Bay Area, focusing primarily on assisting the Chinese women trapped by this situation of slavery. This work began when she was nineteen years of age and first became familiar with the social justice efforts of the Presbyterian Mission House located in San Francisco's Chinatown (Thomas, 2003).

It is believed that over the course of her career, she was able to assist in helping more than three thousand Chinese women escape their enslavement, although the numbers are difficult to confirm because of the hush-hush nature of the situation during the time in which she was performing this important work. Cameron learned much of her skill in this type of work during the time that she was working with the Presbyterian Mission Home. The work was dangerous, involving constant confrontations with slave owners in the area, as well as risky processes for locating slave girls who were frequently found hidden behind the false walls of slave homes (Thomas, 2003). Donaldina Cameron learned skills which ranged from the ability to fight off attackers to the working knowledge of the legal options available to those women who ended up in her care (Thomas, 2003).

Cameron completed this work in a number of locations, but it was her work at the Presbyterian Mission Home which started it all. By the turn of the twentieth century, Donaldina Cameron was superintendent of the home for girls (Thomas, 2003). In 1906, this famous location was destroyed in the earthquake. It is reported that Cameron braved the fires following the earthquake to salvage the legal documents which gave her guardianship rights over some of the girls in her care (Thomas, 2003). It took two years before the home was rebuilt, but it was completed in 1908, and Cameron's work there was resumed.

Perhaps the earthquake's effects were not all bad because when the home was rebuilt, it was able to be done so with an eye towards its intended purpose. Taking into consideration the unique situation of the illegal Chinese slave women, the new house was built with secret passageways and sealed doorways. This would allow the women increased anonymity and at least a sliver of hope that they would be safe until they could move out of the home and into their new American lives.

The basement of the home was designed to be a place where Chinese women, rescued from the slave trade, could have a haven while figuring out what their next move would be. In order to keep the basement room secret, both from slave traders and from the local police, there was no entry into the basement from the inside of the house. There was only the underground passageway which led from a hidden section of the street straight in to the basement of the new house.

For a time, this home was a safe place for these women. They could spend a small or a significant amount of time in the home, moving in and out secretly through the basement, while they figured out how to locate their families and what to do next with their lives. But alas, new tragedy struck the lives of the women who were just beginning to escape their horrid histories. The house caught fire. With no escape except for the underground passage, countless Chinese women died, suffocating in the basement of the home.

In 1939, the home was moved to a location at 142 Wetmore Street (Cameron, 1939). In 1942, the house at 920 Sacramento Street was renamed the Donaldina Cameron House in honor of the woman who is credited with helping to eliminate the slavery of Chinese girls in the city (Thomas, 2003). The original post-quake building stands today as a church and family service agency under this same name and continues to serve the needs of immigrants from China and other parts of Asia. But the dark past of the home remains present. The doors are still sealed, and though there are red and gold charms designed to keep away the evil spirits, it is believed that the ghosts of the women killed in that basement remain in there to this day (S.F. Heart, 2006). Photos taken in the house have shown white figures in the background. People in the home regualarly report experiencing the brush of the home's history via spirits in the house.

Sadly, the ghosts of Chinese women haunting the house are not the only ghosts at this location. Chinese boys, too, may be haunting the home as a result of a mid-twentieth century tragedy which re-ignited the flames of the exploitative past of the home. From 1947 - 1977, the Cameron House was a Presbyterian mission run by Reverand F. S. "Dick" Wichman (Hill, 2006). It is believed that Wichman was a perpetrator of violent sexual abuse against many of the boys in his mission (Hill, 2006). That abuse took place in the very same basement which is said to be haunted by the ghosts of dead slave girls. These were Chinese immigrant boys who were just learning the ways of the Western world and who were taught not to speak against elders, especially revered people such as the Reverand Wicham (Hill, 2006).

Sometimes a location itself cries for the tragedies which have taken place there. San Francisco is rich with cultural diversity and an open acceptance of the many different lifestyles which one may choose to live during the time spent in the area. However, it is also a city where different cultures have spent many years in close quarters and where the opportunity for exploitation and mistreatment of one another has been sometimes increased. The tragedy of the abuse which took place in the home during the mid-twentieth century came at a time which was distinct from the time of that illegal transportation of Chinese women. However, the histories are linked, not only by their similarities but also by their sharing of the San Francisco home on Sacramento Street.

Perhaps the cries that can be heard coming from the basement on lonely nights are the girls crying not only for themselves but also for the victims of the abuse to which they were silent witnesses.

Montandon Townhouse:
A Cursed Home

Lombard Street is famous for being the "crookedest" street in the world. Daily, visitors from all across the globe traipse up to the peak of this glorious San Francisco hill in order to experience one of the wonders for which San Francisco is known. In more recent years, the street also became known as the location of the Real World House San Francisco, increasing traffic to the area by visitors seeking to get a brush with California fame. (The house, which was the home of the Real World cast during the 1994 television season, is located at 949 Lombard Street at the bottom of the crooked part of the hill). Activity bustles here at almost all times. But there is something unsettling happening on Lombard Street which is frequently not known by those who hover around this crooked part of Lombard, taking pictures and relaxing on their vacations.

The trouble seems to have begun in the 1960's, when Pat Montandon (well-known as the author and society girl of her time) moved in to a house on the famous street. The house was located just up the street from what would eventually become the Real World House, across the way and up along the crooked part a bit at the address of 1000 Lombard (Dr. Weirde, 2006). It was a time when astrology was becoming increasingly popular among certain groups in the city, and Montandon, who frequently hosted social gatherings at the Lombard home, threw a party which was themed to this popular event (Haunted Bay, 2006). The party included the presence of a tarot reader who was there to provide information about the pasts and futures to the guests of the party. It should have been all fun and games, but during the reading, something went awry. For reasons unknown, the tarot reader became incredibly agitated and angry with Montandon, reportedly after her failure to properly serve him with a drink (Donat, 2001). During the reading, he faced Montandon and cursed her aloud, saying that he was vexing Montandon as well as the home that she lived in.

It is hard to say whether the number of tragedies in Montandon's life which occurred shortly thereafter have anything to do with the curse. But it is not hard to see that luck was not with her after that time. In fact, Montandon memorialized the events in her second book, *The Intruders,* which was published in 1975 (Donat, 2001). However, before she could do so, she had to live through the difficulties which seemed to come one after another just following the curse. Problems which ensued shortly after the purported curse included the vandalism of her home, the destruction of her car, and even threats on her life. Montandon's reputation become marred with links to numerous affairs and her promising career fell short of its potential (Haunted Bay, 2006). Curse or no curse, her life rapidly became a mess.

The home, too, suffered in the wake of the curse. In 1969, there was a fire in the Montandon Townhouse (Haunted Bay, 2006). The roots of the fire are mysterious and the circumstances which surround the tragedy are almost impossible to explain. At the time, Montandon's best friend, Mary Louise Ward, was staying in the home. When the damage from the fire was over, her dead body was found in the house. Although there is no known reason why she would do so, it appears that perhaps Ward caused the fire, because the front door of the home was chained and barred from the inside and Ward's body was found in a bedroom which was also locked from the inside. Autopsy reports revealed that Ward had been dead before the fire reached her body, but they could not determine a cause of death (Weirde, 2006). In fact, they ruled out every plausible cause of death including burning, smoke inhalation, physical abuse of any kind, and internal organ damage (Haunted Bay, 2006).

Whether or not Ward committed suicide in the home is unknown, but what is known is that two other friends of Montandon's did commit suicide in the house within a short time of one another. Shortly thereafter, signs of spirit activity began to be painfully noticeable. Locked windows would open on their own. A constant chill filled the house. Sounds without sources were not uncommon. Blood stains would appear on the ceiling and grow larger and larger until they suddenly disappeared (Weirde, 2006). Trying to escape the tragedy that was permeating her life, Montandon moved from the location. However, curiosity (and perhaps a need for closure) motivated Montandon to hire two psychics to investigate the activity in the home.

The experts, Gerri Patton and Nick Nocerino, came to the home, having been given no information about the location (Haunted Bay, 2006). Almost immediately upon entrance in to the location, Nocerino relayed the experiences of the home detail-by-detail, including the names and details of those who had died within its walls (Haunted Bay, 2006). After verifying this information, the psychics took photos which, when printed, showed the image of a woman bent over a drawer, her hand raised in surprise as though she had just discovered something from which she was automatically recoiling. The photo, marked with a strange light, differed from the negative of the photo (which did not show the woman at all). Due to skepticism, photos were taken a second time in the presence of witnesses in the home, and the same results occurred.

An exorcism was performed on the house and Montandon moved on with her life. In fact, once Montandon left the cursed home, she fared rather well for herself. She became known around the world for her work with children and her encouragement of peace all throughout the globe, including her creation of a non-profit organization known as "Children as The Peacemakers" (Montandon, 2001). At the beginning of the twentieth century, she was even nominated for a Nobel Peace Prize for this work (Montadon, 2001). However, the effects of the past clearly left a mark on her worldly beliefs, because when asked if she is a religious woman, she will reply that she is metaphysical in her beliefs (Zellerbach, 2001).

Just as Montandon has mostly moved on with her life, so it appears that the Montandon Townhouse is no longer the resting place of the spirits which once made their tragic mark on the home. Those who live at the Lombard Street location today may not even be aware of the tumultuous history of the home, as it is believed that the curse was lifted with the performing of the exorcism (Haunted Bay, 2006). However, when Lombard Street experiences a rare moment of quiet stillness, you can feel a chill in the air there that points to this deeply involved past.

Whittier Mansion:
Extravagance With A Price

William Franklin Whittier. Even the name sounds distinguished. And the stately mansion which was constructed by the man of this distinguished name continues to do justice to the imposing image the name provokes to this very day.

The Whittier Mansion, built in approximately 1895 on a hill in what is now known as the Pacific Heights Neighborhood of San Francisco, is a building with a refined appearance which stands out in contrast with the colorful Victorian architecture for which San Francisco is best known (Haunted Bay, 2006). The Whittier Mansion is made of red sandstone and boasts thirty rooms including a 24' x 32' entrance hall with carved oak paneling, an octagon-shaped smoking room with mahogany paneling, and a 36' x 54' ballroom (NRHSF, 2006). It is 16,000 square feet in size, with thirty rooms spread out over four floors (Haunted Bay, 2006).

In addition to the grandiose design of the rooms of this mansion, the German silver hardware located throughout the house and the towers and gorgeous exterior façade are enhanced historically by the fact that the Whittier Mansion was the first ever location to be designed with a stone structure over a steel frame, a design which eventually become frequently used in the area and throughout the world (NRHSF, 2006). The Whittier Mansion is truly an icon of architectural genius, and it is a place which has stood out in the area since it was first constructed.

Who was the man behind the construction of such an elegant location? Whittier was a local businessman who made his fortune by dipping his finger into the trades of being a merchant, a shipper, and a railroader. Although it sounds like only pennies today, the $152,000 price tag on the mansion was a lot of money back when it was first constructed, money which Whittier could easily toss around since he was one of the Bay Area's first millionaires (Olmsted, et. al., 1969).

But money couldn't save Whittier's life from distress. The mansion was created as a gift for his wife, a woman with whom he was desperately in love, a woman to whom he wanted to give the world. Surely, she would have appreciated the magnificence of this gift. Had she lived. However, such was not to be the Whittier fate. Just before the completion of the mansion's construction, Mrs. Whittier was involved in a carriage accident which ended in her death (Olmsted, 1969).

Whittier probably struggled for awhile with the decision of whether or not to move in to the mansion after all, given that his wife had never even seen its final beauty, but he ultimately made the decision to go ahead and live in the house without her. He moved in to the home with his son, Billy, a man who was known around town primarily for his carousing and his immature behavior (Olmsted, 1969). Billy made use of the elaborate resources earned by his father to carve out a life of luxury for himself. In modern day terms, Billy would be known as a silver-spoon baby who turned into a slacker.

Billy and his father did not spend a significant amount of time talking with one another. They had an uneasy relationship which was spent primarily trying to avoid dealing with one another too closely. They lived mostly quiet lives, each playing the strong, silent type as they tried to work out the feelings over the death of Mrs. Whittier. Mr. Whittier died in the home in 1917. Billy remained until the late 1930s (Olmsted, 1969).

The interesting history of the Whittier mansion does not end when the Whittiers were no longer a part of its life. In 1940, the Whittier mansion was acquired by the German government for use as their German consulate (NRHSF, 2006). Historical associations with the location related to this time include events hosted by Adolph Hitler's commanding officer, Fritz Wiedemann, and his eventual burning of all secret papers in the furnace of the mansion which took place at the beginning of the Second World War (Olmsted, 1969).

After extensive investigation of the mansion stemming from this association with Germany during wartime, the home was acquired by the Mortimer Adler Institute for Philosophical Research, and then moved on to being the home of the California Historical Society (NRHSF, 2006). At the present time, it has returned to being a private home. It is clearly a home with a rich history.

And perhaps the Whittiers were never quite able to leave behind the physical gem of their lives. To this day, one or both of the male Whittiers haunts the mansion. The basement is said to always have an icy chill and there is frequently seen there the shadowy outline of a male figure (Haunted Bay, 2006). Most people believe that it is the elder Mr. Whittier who has remained behind in the home which he constructed for the love that he lost. But some say that it is actually the younger Mr. Billy Whittier who is still enjoying the fruits of his father's success by bothering the guests of the home in which he indulged in the good life throughout his living years (Hauck, 2006).

Part II:
Hotels

Understandably, those who lived their lives in San Francisco may want to remain around the area. They have unfinished business to attend to, or perhaps they simply loved the luxury of their lives too much to want to leave it all behind. But those who owned homes and thrived in the city are not the only ones whose spirits linger in the heart of San Francisco. In fact, in many cases, it is those people whose lives were lived elsewhere who seem to have come, in the end, to settle in San Francisco.

Many of these people were the movers and shakers of the literary and social worlds of the nineteenth and early twentieth centuries. San Francisco was a hotbed for activity during this time, and numerous famous people came to the area to indulge in the bohemian lifestyle allowed by the city. These times are associated with splendor and perhaps hedonism, a mixture of the merry and the melancholy. For this reason, many of the hotels of the area are said to be haunted, possibly by the spirits of the people who made San Francisco their home away from home.

In addition to the draw of the city itself, hotels of the area had a particular appeal for the charming lifestyle enjoyed by the elite of society, especially during the Prohibition Era, because of their association with hosting high-end bars. Most hotels had bars in the lobby from the time that they were constructed, and many of these became underground speakeasies during the period of historical time when alcohol was made illegal throughout the United States.

Spirits tend to form during dynamic circumstances, and the excitement of the speakeasies was nothing if not dynamic! It is often said that one may leave the city of San Francisco, but the heart will be left behind. And so it is not really difficult to believe that the celebrities and socialites who graced the hotels around the city and who imbibed the drinks of the Prohibition era in the speakeasies scattered throughout the underground world of the time, have returned to the area to enjoy the memories of days past in the place where they once lost their hearts.

Empire Plush Room Cabaret:
Prohibition's Piano Player

Ghosts are associated with enjoying trouble, and although this is not always the case (as many ghosts are apparently harmless), there does seem to be a link between actively troubled times and the development of the presence of spirits. Sometimes, such troubled times are related to serious tragedy (as is the case with those spirits said to have unfinished business which they are working out in their deaths). But in other cases, the trouble is a more fun-filled, prankster kind of trouble which leaves the people who experienced the activity of a certain time and place some desire to never leave the fun behind.

This is the case with the haunting of the Empire Plush Room Cabaret, a bar and lounge which is located at 940 Sutter Street. Although still active as a nightlife location today, the time during which real activity thrived in this location was the early 1920s. At that time, The Empire Plush Room was a part of a short-term accommodations location known as the York Hotel. The people who frequented the York Hotel were those exciting out-of-towners who were in San Francisco for weekends or holidays, as well as those people from the area who were interested in getting themselves engaged in a little bit of scandalous fun.

Prohibition was raging strong at that point in time, and a vast number of speakeasies opened up in San Francisco to accommodate the thirst for alcohol which didn't go away just because the law said that it should. The York Hotel was one of those locations. The hotel itself was operated legitimately, of course, but within the hotel was a secret room where the luxurious imbibing of forbidden drinks could be enjoyed by those who didn't have qualms about engaging in a little bit of illicit behavior.

To reach the secret room, guests would enter a hidden door and travel through underground passageways, an architectural design trait which was common in the area at the time (May, 2004). They would eventually reach a plush room, the décor of which lent itself easily to the name by which the location was known. San Francisco socialites of the area frequently made this trek trough the underground passageways. They would gather together to gossip (and to create reasons for others to gossip), drinking the free-flowing liquor and watching nightly entertainment (May, 2004). It was an exciting time when the taboo nature of the activity increased the pleasure of the fun for everyone involved.

Nightly, the plush room of the York Hotel would glitter with the sparkling laughter of those people who were enjoying life together in this secret world. The soundtrack for this scene was live piano music, something which was greatly enjoyed in the speakeasies all throughout San Francisco. The piano player at the Plush Room, a man known as Lester, was revered in speakeasy circles of his day for his talent on the instrument as well as for his abundant personality which added to the fun of the nightly events (May, 2004).

But not all was fun and games. To the horror of the socialites and those who mingled with them, there was one night when Lester was playing the piano, demonstrating his full glory, when he suddenly keeled over and died (May, 2004). Although the speakeasy would remain open through Prohibition, there was a somber tune which filled the air for a long time after Lester's death.

It is said that Lester was one of those lucky people who died doing what he loved the most. And perhaps Lester didn't want to leave behind the fun of the glory days when his piano-playing skills created the mood for which the York Hotel was famous in the underground scene, because it seems that Lester never left the Empire Plush Room. Even after Prohibition ended and the room became open to the public once again, Lester couldn't seem to let the old days go. To this day, staff working at the Empire Plush Room Cabaret frequently say that they can hear piano music emanating out of the empty room (May, 2004).

Hotel Union Square:
Hellman's Home Away From Home

It is not uncommon for more than one ghost to linger in a location, and it is also not uncommon for one ghost out of the group to take precedence over all of the others, demanding attention and encouraging the other spirits in their activities. This is because there are locations which seem to draw in the spirits of numerous people, perhaps because of something dynamic about their character. As in life, so in death—there will often be a leader of the ghost group who stands out above all of the others making their home in a particular area, in the same way that leaders tend to emerge spontaneously when groups of people come together during their waking lives. The Hotel Union Square may be one of those locations where numerous lost souls return after life has ended, and Lillian Hellman just may be one of those spirits who dominates the haunted location.

The Hotel Union Square is another one of those locations which was home to a speakeasy during the Prohibition Era. Guests who wished to indulge in the imbibing of alcohol would enter through a side door and remain in the hallway on that end of the hotel where they could carouse without getting caught. Today, guests walking through that hallway often see drunken bodies laughing and lying on the floor, although when they approach, the bodies disappear. Reported sightings of spirits of many kinds are common by guests of the hotel. But the one who seems to show up most often is Lillian Hellman.

There is a word for the spirit of Lillian Hellman when she was alive. In fact, there are several words. Moxie. Chutzpah. Chispa. No matter what the language, these words attempt to encapsulate the fiery spirit of a person who lives a life filled with sass and vigor and passion. And though Lillian Hellman can't be summed up with just a single word, the concept of what those definitions try to convey wrapped itself through every moment of Hellman's life.

Perhaps that spirit was bred into her through her unique upbringing. Born in the vivid city of New Orleans, Hellman spent her childhood moving back and forth between that home and a second home in the even more vibrant New York City (Kirjasto, 2006). She developed her career as a playwright, simultaneously developing an intimate relationship with author Dashiel Hammett which would be described today as a "friends-with-benefits" situation (Kirjasto, 2006).

Such a situation was not common at the time that Lillian Hellman and Dashiel Hammett entered into it, but Hellman was not one to let convention stop her from figuring out which situations in life best suited her and pursuing them wholeheartedly. She would have affairs with several men throughout her life, but her primarily emotional and sexual relationship was with Hammett, and her primary commitment was to her career as a writer (Kirjasto, 2006).

The relationship that Hellman and Hammett shared was as dynamic as their individual lives were. Both were well-traveled authors and both were involved in liberal activities which marked them as Communists during an era when such a word could barely pass through the lips of the every day person without a sneer. Both Hellman and Hammett refused to cooperate with the House of Representatives Committee on Un-American activities (Kirjasto, 2006). Hammett served time for his non-compliance, but the committee released Hellman because she was considered non-threatening due primarily to the fact that she was female (Kirjasto, 2006).

Hellman may not have been threatening to the men of Congress at the time, but her fiery spirit was never easily tamed. She lived her life with a kind of reckless abandon which suggested that she was going to enjoy every single minute that she possibly could. And that she did. It is believed that, just before her death in 1984, when she was on the verge of turning eighty years old, she propositioned a much younger man to enjoy an affair (Kirjasto, 2006). That was the kind of woman that Hellman was in her life.

A life lived with such abandon is bound to have some regrets. It is hard to say what Hellman's were, because she lived with such passion and desire to keep moving forward that her regrets are diminished to the point of near-oblivion. But it is possible that, in her later years, she wished that she had had spent even more time with Dashiel Hammett than she did.

The belief in this possibility stems from the fact that Hellman, though a world traveler, seems to have returned in death to the spot where she and Hammett had their most frequent affairs. Hellman and Hammett were well-known at the Hotel Union Square, where they carried out their intimate friendship on more than one occasion. Perhaps in longing for the passion of those days, Hellman's spirit is said to haunt the Hotel Union Square.

Room 207 is the one in which she is most frequently seen (May, 2004). Small objects will appear in the room, a Kleenex that she left behind for example, but she never bothers the guests who are coming to visit her (May, 2004). She is friendly in her death, opening and closing the door to the room as though she just wants to come in and out again in the hopes of finding her lover there waiting for her as he once did.

But perhaps Hellman is looking in the wrong location, because Hammett is also reported to have returned to the Bay Area during his death, but it is not the Hotel Union Square which he seems to have made his home. Instead, it is the Flood Building. And maybe there is something which speaks to the dynamism of this dashing couple, because—as with the Hotel Union Square—the Flood Building is said to be haunted by many people, not just the man who has made its history most famous.

Prior to becoming known as the Flood Building, the building which stood on the same site was the Baldwin Hotel. The fancy accommodations of this location included a swimming pool and skating rink used by guests as well as by the San Francisco public. The laughter of the playing children in those spots was cut short one day in 1898 when, like so many other buildings in the area at the time, a fire broke out and the Baldwin Hotel burned down. Numerous lives were lost to the fire (Flood Building, 2006).

In 1904, the Flood Building was constructed over the site of the Baldwin Hotel (Flood Building, 2006). From the time that it was erected, it was said that the cries of those who died in the fire could be heard on occasional nights. Nevertheless, the Flood Building thrived as a central location in the Financial District of the bustling city. One of the many businesses to be housed in the new location was the Pinkerton Detective Agency, the employer of Dashiell Hammett (Flood Building, 2006).

Today, if you take the stairs between the third floor and the fourth floor of the Flood Building, and you pause long enough, you may be able to feel the chill in the air which is said to be the ghost of Dashiell Hammett. If you listen closely, you may be able to hear the tunes of 1930s-style music playing lightly in the background (May, 2004). And if you close your eyes and pay close enough attention, perhaps you can conjure up the image of Hammett himself, waiting in the Flood Building for his friend and lover who is doing the same thing over at Hotel Union Square.

Perhaps Hammett will get wind of the fact that the Hotel Union Square has created a room in his honor and he will make his way over there to find his lost love. However, there could be trouble in deadly paradise if that is the case because the hotel advertises that Hammett's affection for the location was not because of his associations there with Hellman, but rather because of the pre-wedding night that he spent there with his eventual bride, Josephine Dolan (Hotel Union Square, 2006).

Queen Anne Hotel:
A Teacher Makes History

The Queen Anne Hotel is located at 1590 Sutter Street, where Sutter intersects with Octavia. Today, it is a Victorian-style hotel dating back to the late nineteenth century, a stunning piece of architecture which captures the eyes of passersby and the hearts of those who come to San Francisco to experience the type of historic homes which make the area distinct from the rest of California. However, appearances can be deceiving, and this frosting-pink gem of a beautiful building holds more within its walls than just the interior design of a magnificent hotel.

Indeed, this place where the accommodations are attractive enough to draw in visitors from all across the world is also the location which at least one woman has decided is a place that she never wants to leave. Although the Queen Anne has been a hotel for a little while now, it has also been a number of other types of buildings during past lifetimes. One of the organizations once held within the building, back in the nineteenth century when it was first constructed, was a girls' boarding school named Miss Mary Lake's School for Young Ladies, after the educator who headed the school (Crawford, 2002).

Mary Lake was an educator who was committed to providing a quality education for girls during a time when girls were not generally educated to be anything more than the wives of successful (or not so successful!) men. Despite her strong hand in the educating of the girls who would pass through her school's hallways, the educational institution which bore her name was built without her input. The building was constructed by Senator James Graham Fair, probably as a means of moving his two daughters closer to him in the city without actually having to take them into his own home (Crawford, 2002). But perhaps Miss Lake actually had more input than many initially thought, because it is believed that she was not only the superintendent of the school but also the mistress of the man who had the school built (Whitington, 2001).

Although education of women was quite different than it is now, Mary Lake was devoted to doing the best that she could to broaden the minds of the daughters of Senator Fair, as well as the minds of all of her other young subjects. As a woman of her times, Mary Lake taught her students all of the arts of being a refined lady. In effect, the girls' school was a finishing school. However, Mary Lake also taught her girls a basic foundation of study in general subjects so that they could be prepared for whatever life might throw at them during the changing times (Whitington, 2001).

Unfortunately, Mary Lake was ahead of her time. The school closed down due to a combination of factors, including a lack of support and unavailability of resources (Crawford, 2002). Mary Lake is said to have never recovered from the loss and she died just a few short years after the school had opened its doors. Apparently, she never found a better place than the location of the school to spend her days.

The school closed before the turn of the twentieth century, and the building spent most of that century changing ownership again and again. At some periods of time, it was a private residence. At other periods of time, it was a place of business. At one point in time, it was even the place of gathering for a secret society with activities related to the science of astrology (Whitington, 2001). In 1980, it became the Queen Anne Hotel, a business which has thrived ever since that opening day (Crawford, 2002).

In spite of the fact that more than a century of time has passed and the building has undergone so many different changes with so many different faces passing through, it is said that Miss Mary Lake never left the location behind. Visitors spending time in Room 410 of the Queen Anne Hotel have reported frequent sightings of the lost school teacher (Whitington, 2001). This room is the location of what was originally Mary Lake's office in the girls' school (Whitington, 2001).

Reports by people who have experienced the ghosts in this room indicate that, despite the presence of chilling cold spots, the overall sense that they receive from the ghost is that she is a warm and loving presence who is merely there to watch out for the guests of the hotel, a location which she simply could not bear to leave behind. On one occasion, a guest reported that he had fallen easily to sleep upon returning to the room and was woken up later to discover that he had been lovingly tucked in beneath the covers (Whitington, 2001).

Novice ghost hunters who have a strong interest in learning more about how their lives can be touched by spirits, but who also have something of a fear of the idea of actually beginning to do so, may find that the Queen Anne Hotel offers a happy medium for their initial exploration into this new world. Of all of the ghost stories told throughout the history and region of San Francisco, it is the one of Miss Mary Lake at the Queen Anne Hotel which seems to never be related as a story of fear. Yes, it may still be a little bit disarming to experience a connection with this ghost, but she is widely considered by those who have felt her presence to be a benevolent spirit who is unlikely to cause any harm. She isn't even reported to pull silly pranks on guests like some other spirits across time and place are accused of doing. Because of this, and because of the ease of booking a room at the still-operating Queen Anne Hotel, this makes an excellent location for trying to create a true ghost story of your own.

The staff of the Queen Anne Hotel is reported to be as friendly as the ghost of Miss Mary Lake. Those who work at the Queen Anne are happy to help others gain experience of ghostly action during their stay in the hotel. In fact, the lobby of the Queen Anne Hotel is the starting point for a nightly ghost tour (The San Francisco Ghost Hunt) which is led by Jim Fassbinder, a San Francisco local expert on the ghosts of the area. Beginning with an introduction to the friendly ghost who walks the floors of the Queen Anne, this tour then goes on to explore areas around the hotel which are also said to be haunted, mostly by ghosts who are said to be not nearly as friendly as Miss Mary Lake!

They say that teachers make a mark on history all of the time, leaving their impressions upon young minds in ways which affect both the present and the future, but it appears that the spirit of Mary Lake is making at least as much of an impression in death as the woman she was did during her lifetime.

Hotel Majestic:
Milton Schmidt's Restless Daughter

Although the Hotel Majestic is reported to be one of the longest running hotels in the city of San Francisco, it was originally not a hotel at all but rather a private residence, built right at the turn of the twentieth century as the home of Milton Schmidt, a California government representative (Hotel Majestic Home Page, 2006). Schmidt only lived in the home for two years, though, before he moved to a new residence and the location became the Majestic Hotel. This took place just before the 1906 earthquake, and the Hotel Majestic was one of the few buildings in the location which survived the damage of that tragic time. This gives it a special place in the hearts of San Franciscans and in the history of San Francisco.

However, this is not all that makes the Hotel Majestic stand out among the other buildings of the area. The hotel's frequent brushes with the spirit side of the world also make it a notable location in San Francisco history. There are numerous different spirits which seem to linger in this Pacific Heights location, haunting those who stay in the hotel during trips to the city for business or for pleasure (Hotel Majestic Home Page, 2006).

The fourth floor seems to be the location where the ghosts like to linger, walking down the hallway late at night and waking up hotel guests with the sound of keys clanking on a large key ring (Hotel Majestic Home Page, 2006). There is one room (Room 406) in which the bathtub frequently fills up with water although no one (visible) has been around to turn the water on (Hotel Majestic Home Page, 2006).

Among the more famous stories circulating about experiences of hauntings in the Hotel Majestic is the story of a guest who was staying in the hotel while working on the set of the film "Sweet November" (Hotel Majestic Home Page, 2006). In the middle of the night, she approached the front desk, asking if there had been an earthquake. The person working the front desk must have given her a bewildered look, as there was neither an earthquake nor any sign of an earthquake. The guest explained that her bed had been shaking. The shaking was attributed to the ghosts who haunt the location (Hotel Majestic Home Page, 2006).

It is believed that the ghost, or at least one of the ghosts, as there may be many at the Hotel Majestic, is Milton Schmidt's daughter, who simply did not want to leave the home when her father moved on (Hotel Majestic Home Page, 2006). Today, a portrait of her stands in the lobby of the hotel, offering her a sign of peace that the staff and guests of the hotel are willing to continue to accommodate her as long as she remains the harmless spirit that she has so far been reported to be.

Mansions Hotel:
The Chambers In Your Chambers

The Mansions Hotel, located at 2220 Sacramento Street, consists of two different mansions combined together to make one hotel. Guests who stay in the newer of the two mansions sleep with relative ease and comfort, enjoying the luxury of the accommodations. The accommodations may be just as pleasant in the older mansion of the hotel, but there is restlessness in the air there. It is believed that numerous spirits linger in the ancient rooms of this spot, but there is one in particular who simply will not go away. In fact, she is so bothersome that perhaps she has brought ill will to the mansion, which has recently been converted from a hotel to private condos.

Claudia Chambers was the niece of Richard Chambers, a man who made his fortune during the late nineteenth century by mining for silver. Although his fortune was made in the state of Utah, Chambers was in love with the city of San Francisco, and when he could afford to do so, he built his mansion there. In 1901, Richard Chambers passed away, leaving the mansion to Claudia and a second niece. The girls never got along and the second niece ultimately built the second mansion next door to the original home.

Claudia remained in the original mansion where she died in a strange accident. The accident and the circumstances surrounding the accident were, in fact, so strange that there is disagreement throughout history as to what exactly took place. Some say that there were knives involved, that she was stabbed to death in a story which doesn't describe who or how this occurred. Others say that she was sawed in half during the course of mysterious events. The official newspaper report of her death says that she was killed in a "farm implementation accident" (Whitington, 2001).

In 1977, the mansion was purchased by Bob Pritkin who turned it into the Mansions Hotel and Restaurant (May, 2006). His renovation of the building was astounding and travelers flocked from all around the world to see what he had done with this location. But Claudia Chambers was none too happy with the change. Guests of the hotel and restaurant reported numerous problems with ghost activity including the sudden ripping off of a toilet seat from its hinge, the explosion of wine glasses on numerous occasions, and even the dropping of a large heavy door onto one unfortunate guest (May, 2006).

Throughout the time that the hotel was in operation, Pritkin repeatedly insisted that it was impossible that the place was haunted, because he simply did not believe in ghost activity. However, after numerous sightings of the ghost of Claudia Chambers, including his own experience with seeing her image appear in the dinner plate from which he was eating, Pritkin reportedly came to accept that her spirit must be in the place, and that there was little to nothing that he was aware of that he could do to get rid of her ghost (May, 2006). It was at least, in part, as a result of this activity that Pritkin eventually opted to sell the hotel.

Before being converted in to condos, the Mansions Hotel was a part of the famous San Francisco Ghost Hunt Tour conducted by Jim Fassbinder. This certified ghost hunter let curiosity get the best of him and did his own research into the death of Claudia Chambers. What could not be revealed in life is said to have been determined in death. Fassbinder reportedly believes that Claudia was a victim at the hands of another member of the family. The family member was considered to be crazy and was locked in the attic of the mansion. Escaping one day, the crazy relative chased Claudia down the stairs, into the Josephine Room of the mansion and murdered her with a knife.

Patrons of the famous San Francisco hotel have seen numerous different ghosts on a variety of occasions. Televisions will turn on without human assistance. Toilets will flush without any living person in the bathroom. A book has been reported as flying across the room in the Presidential Suite. A man once stumbled down to the lobby, shaking and pale-faced. He wouldn't say what had happened, but he insisted that he had to leave the hotel immediately (Hauck, 2006).

The Mansions Hotel is a rich part of San Francisco history, and it is one which is true to San Francisco nature in that it changes with the times. No longer a hotel, the building was sold in 2000 and has been reconstructed to create private condos (May, 2004). Perhaps the renovations have finally driven out the persistent Ms. Chambers. Or perhaps she's just waiting for the right moment to let the new tenants of the building know that the place was hers first and she's not giving it up easily.

Westin St. Francis:
The Place To See and Be Seen

The Westin St. Francis is a glorious hotel situated in the heart of San Francisco, located just across from the bustling activity of Union Square and close to the ongoing action of San Francisco's main street, Market Street. In addition to the guests who come to enjoy the deluxe accommodations of this grandiose hotel, locals and travelers alike stop in to enjoy the restaurants, private parties, and upscale shopping offered within the lobby of the location. People also often visit the hotel simply to take a few spare moments to ride the glass elevator to the top floor, looking out through its windows to the astounding view of the eastern side of the city and the East Bay which lies below the towering building.

The Westin St. Francis was first built in 1904, but it had been in the process of being designed for more than two years prior to that. An immense amount of work went into the planning of the hotel which was created with the intention of making it the "finest hotel on the Pacific Coast" in the hopes of helping San Francisco become something like a "Paris of the West" (Westin St. Francis, 2006). Its design is an amalgamation of styles from all of the major hotels in Europe at the time, giving it a distinctly cosmopolitan flavor which is what San Francisco is all about.

The effort (and money, with an initial price tag of two and a half million dollars) that went into creating this hotel was well worth it—from day one, the place was a draw for big names in the San Francisco scene. On opening day, the line to get in was three blocks in length (Westin St. Francis, 2006). Within six months, the Westin St. Francis was one of the most talked about locations in the area's artistic and literary circles. Socialites flocked to the accommodations in such droves that plans immediately began for expanding the hotel to include two floors of apartments, a ballroom, and additional rental rooms (Westin St. Francis, 2006).

However, 1906 happened and history left its mark. The experience of the earthquake at the Westin St. Francis was an interesting one. The quake itself did very little damage to the glorious hotel. As people wandered around Union Square in a daze, the hotel remained in operation. Guests were unscathed. In fact, it is said that famous name John Barrymore had been out and about and he returned to the comfort of the well-known hotel to enjoy his bed there (May, 2004). He was startled awake by the alarm warning everyone to get out of the building immediately.

The warning came because, although the quake didn't damage the structure of the building, the fires which followed were highly destructive. One of the favored stories of the hotel's historians is that, although the fire wreaked havoc throughout the building, a return to the building after the fire had ended found the pet dog of the hotel's wine steward alive in the basement of the hotel (Westin St. Francis, 2006). The dog immediately became a symbol for the hotel's ability to survive anything, and work commenced on rebuilding the magnificent location.

It took just over a year and a half for the hotel to re-open, but when it did, it met the same degree of success as it had in its first two years of operation. Famous names floated in and out of the building as easily as ghosts move through the walls of some rooms. Barrymore returned to enjoy the hotel on a number of occasions. He was a theatre actor at the time, but quickly went on to his screen debut (in 1914) and enjoyed the success of the movie industry, funneling at least a portion of his earnings into nights at the Westin St. Francis (Morrison, 2006).

Another famous name who regularly graced the halls of the rebuilt Westin St. Francis was Edith Pope. She spent much of the 1930s and 1940s living in one of the apartments which became part of the eventual design of the hotel (May, 2004). Edith, and people like her, could spend their time in San Francisco, soaking up the pleasures of the parties and the inspiration of the city and enjoying numerous liaisons and brushes with entertainment at locations like the Westin St. Francis.

But not all of the famous nights spent at the Westin St. Francis were pleasant ones. For example, although Al Jolson (referred to by some as "The World's Greatest Entertainer) had a great time at the hotel on a number of occasions, he also left a sad mark on the spot (International Al Jolson Society, 2006). Al Jolson had a fifty-year-long career in the theatre and music industry of America, including stage work, well-known blackface appearances, and work in eleven feature films (International Al Jolson Society, 2006). He moved across America, touching the hearts of numerous people with his lilting voice and his ability to keep others entertained.

Al Jolson regularly wound up in San Francisco. Sometimes he was in the city to perform in various entertainment activities. On other occasions, he was in San Francisco for purposes of pure vacation, taking a rest from the hustle and bustle of his life by enjoying the excellent service of hotels, which frequently included the Westin St. Francis. He enjoyed many a night in the famous location and there are people around with good memories of the times that he spent there. But in 1950, while playing poker in Suite 1221 of the hotel, he passed on from this side of life (May, 2004). Perhaps the Westin St. Francis was not only his favorite resting place, but also his final one.

Jolson's death was one which was certainly sad and which affected the lives of those at the hotel at the time. However, it was not a tragic death. The Westin St. Francis, however, has seen at least one of those, the most well-known of which is associated with another famous name: Roscoe Fatty Arbuckle. Roscoe, a famous figure in the world of silent cinema (who got his name from the fact that he weighed a whopping fourteen pounds at birth and carried that kind of girth throughout his lifetime) was also present in the city during the 1906 earthquake, but this is not the only experience which intertwined his personal history with some of the horrors which San Francisco has seen (Pearson, 2005).

In fact, it was fifteen years later that the tragedy for which Al Jolson would become associated with occurred, and it took place at the Westin St. Francis. It was

Labor Day, 1921 (Pearson, 2005). Arbuckle was at the hotel throwing a party to celebrate the end of the filming of "Life of the Party", at which a young actress by the name of Virginia Rappe fell terribly ill and subsequently died. The facts of the event are murky and have been muddled over time by changing accounts of the story by the people who were present at the hotel party.

What is known about that night is that Virginia Rappe came to the party at the Westin St. Francis, where she consumed some amount of alcohol and eventually fell ill from undetermined causes. She passed out at the party, and concerned guests, including Arbuckle, attended to her until she was passed off to the care of the friend with whom she had arrived at the hotel, a woman by the name of Maude Delmont (Pearson, 2005). Arbuckle is reported to have left the party prior to the departure of the two women; due perhaps in large part to the fact that Rappe was not immediately hospitalized, she died four days after the party from complications of peritonitis (Pearson, 2005).

Those are the facts of what happened that night. Varying versions add additional details which tarnished the reputation of Roscoe "Fatty" Arbuckle forever after. His version of the events was that he went from the party to his adjoining bedroom suite to change his clothes, at which time and place he discovered the passed out body of the actress Rappe (Pearson, 2005). Arbuckle reportedly picked her up and placed her on the bed, which she promptly fell out of requiring his additional assistance. He provided her with a glass of water and went back to the party in the adjoining room to get assistance for the problem (Pearson, 2005).

The guests of the party, drunk with celebration, stumbled around Rappe for awhile, trying to figure out how to help her. Eventually, it was determined that Rappe was in need of medical assistance. The management of the Westin St. Francis was summoned, and they assisted Roscoe in moving her body to rest in a nearby room (Room 1227), where she was to be watched over by Maude Delmont who apparently passed out on the adjoining bed awaiting the arrival of a doctor who had been called to the scene (Pearson, 2005). Roscoe is said to have left the Westin St. Francis after the arrival of the doctor (Pearson, 2005).

After four days in the hospital, Virginia Rappe died. At that time, Maude Delmont approached the local authorities and told a quite different version of the events which had taken place at the Westin St. Francis. She accused Roscoe "Fatty" Arbuckle of raping Virginia Rappe and ultimately causing her death. Based on these charges, Arbuckle was arrested for murder (Pearson, 2005). Ultimately, Arbuckle was acquitted of these charges based on the fact that there was no evidence and that the only purported witness to the event—Maude Delmont—repeatedly changed her story as to what took place (Pearson, 2005).

However, in spite of being found innocent, the tragedy was to affect Arbuckle's life forever. He was blacklisted from Hollywood for eleven years following the incident and the public would forever associate him not with all of his many accomplishments, but with the scandal for which he became famous across the nation (Pearson, 2005). To this day, when information about Arbuckle is presented, it rarely fails to mention this tragic time of his life.

And despite the number of wonderful nights which Roscoe "Fatty" Arbuckle is known to have enjoyed at the Westin St. Francis, it will always be this one tragic time which is most associated with his stays at the well-known hotel. Despite these negative associations, the hotel thrived both then and now. With all of this interesting activity taking place and all of these famous names passing through the many floors of the building, it is no wonder that the famous people who enjoyed the hotel during their lives have not all left the hotel.

The Westin St. Francis is reported to have more well-known ghosts than any other location in San Francisco. It is practically a place of congregation for the people of the past whose lives glittered and sparkled and fell short of their potential during the times when they stayed at the hotel. Travelers interested in the rich history of the well-known visitors of San Francisco may find it easy to feel as though they have been transported back in time when they get the opportunity to spend a night or two within the Westin St. Francis accommodations.

The hotel is said to be the resting place of all of these famous names. Edith Pope is believed to be seen floating throughout the St. Francis Suite, wearing a flowing white dress and enjoying her afterlife in the same beautiful manner with which she enjoyed her waking days (May, 2004). John Barrymore continues trying to end his restless nights with a warm bed at the favored hotel. Jolson has reportedly been sighted there as well, although a séance held by the Al Jolson Society turned up no report of him (International Al Jolson Society, 2006).

And of course, there is Roscoe "Fatty" Arbuckle. In spite of his years of being blacklisted by Hollywood, he went on to spend the latter part of his life continuing to make movies, involving himself in the nightclubbing business and marrying a series of women with whom he was supposedly deeply in love (Pearson, 2005). Arbuckle was a man who loved to party, and when he died in 1933, it was as a result of heart failure which occurred after a night spent celebrating one of his many successes (Pearson, 2005).

But perhaps he never quite escaped the painful years of his life which were caused by the problems taking place on the fateful night at the Westin St. Francis in 1921. Perhaps his grandiose spirit is still up on that twelfth floor of the hotel, trying to enjoy the party life that ended so badly that night. The hotel is an active one today, with people coming in and out of the rooms at all times of the day and night, but those who happen to catch a moment of silence in the halls there have found that the building—particularly that twelfth floor where Arbuckle's party and Jolson's poker game both took place—is haunted by the spirits of people from all over the globe.

The nightlife of San Francisco glitters with the glamour of modern adventures as well as the warm history of the number of people who have moved through the scene in the city. It is no wonder that people who once enjoyed an active life in the midst of all of this entertainment don't want to leave the source of their greatest enjoyment. It is also no wonder that, even when times were tragic, the home of San Francisco was comfortable enough for people seeking a place to return to in their deaths. The Westin St. Francis offers a place for both the dead and the living to experience the amazing center of San Francisco in a way simply not to be had anywhere else in the city.

Part III:
Military

When one thinks of tragedy in the Bay Area, it is the earthquakes of the region which first come to mind. The 1906 earthquake and its resulting fires, along with the 1989 earthquake left the mark on the history of the area in ways which other tragedies throughout time simply did not quite do. People think of world events which relate to San Francisco, and these are the things that they think of first.

However, San Francisco is a location which is interlinked with the global environment. Receiving tourists daily from international locations and welcoming in transplants from all around the world, San Francisco stays in touch with the things which are happening in other areas. The events, both small and large, which take place in various locales throughout the world, are noted by the people of San Francisco with interest and concern.

One of the ways in which any place is affiliated with the global scene is through its military connections. Although military presence is not strong in the San Francisco area today, there was a time when active forts were common in the region. And although the military itself tends to be somewhat conservative in its outspoken beliefs about the spirit world, there is little doubt in the minds of many San Franciscans that the old historic homes and buildings of the military there are haunted.

Army Hospital:
Abandoned But Not Empty

Military men are not supposed to be men who get scared. They see death, they see disaster … at the very least, they see the angry faces of their boot camp instructor on a regular enough basis to eradicate any tendencies towards easy fright. However, the Abandoned Army Hospital in Park Presidio has been known to cause fright to more than one Army man, even if he might act too tough to actually admit to it.

The military hospital was the site of a number of tragic deaths (S.F. Heart, 2006). Soldiers who were wounded in the line of duty failed to make recoveries from their injuries and lost their lives within the walls of this old hospital. It is impossible to determine which of those bodies decided to remain active within those walls and which moved on to happier places, but there is little doubt among believers in ghosts that plenty of those spirits remained behind, forever trapped within the once-sterile walls of the long-ago hospital environment.

The building, located inside of the Presidio at the very northern tip of 15th Avenue, was constructed at the end of the nineteenth century for use as a United States Military Hospital (StrangeUSA.com, 2006). In 1931, the building was taken over, demolished, and reconstructed for use as the Public Health Service Hospital; it remained such until 1981, when it was closed down after a half-century of use (StrangeUSA.com, 2006). During that time, countless souls died at the location, some of which perhaps were unable to ever leave.

For the next seven years, the old military hospital was used by the Defense Language Institute (StrangeUSA.com, 2006). However, in spite of the fact that the hospital building was primarily used for non-medical activity at this time, the 6th floor southwest was used by the Letterman Army Medical Center for the execution of animal experimentation and other medical research (StrangeUSA.com, 2006). Some would say that this type of activity created a vortex of pain through which anguished spirits might become entrapped in the area. More macabre individuals might suggest that the devilish ghosts who felt that their lives were unduly disrupted by the terror of their deaths in the hospital might take solace in the dark activity involved in such experimentation and may have found their way to that floor of the abandoned location in order to indulge in the pain of other creatures.

Whatever the case may be, the building's history of death and disease along with the seven-year period of animal experimentation which took place there set the tone for the building to be seen by many as a place with a dark past. In 1988, the building was abandoned entirely (StrangeUSA.com, 2006). And abandonment creates room for the non-living to find a place to spend their days.

In the twenty first century, the Army Hospital became entirely inaccessible. Boards were placed on the windows. A fence was erected around the property. San Francisco Police Department authorities regularly patrol the area and will ticket anyone who is caught trying to trespass (S.F. Heart, 2006). But are those authorities really trying to keep people from entering the property or are they monitoring those who won't leave?

People who have gotten past the authorities and trespassed here have described an eerie setting. Glass litters the ground where windows have been broken, drafts flood through the walls, and footsteps echo (StrangeUSA.com, 2006). The hospital is enormous, consisting of six different buildings which are six to seven stories in height, and it appears even larger than it actually is when there is no one in the building to fill this vast amount of space with sound (StrangeUSA.com, 2006). Especially when you know the fact that the abandoned location means that there is no one but you in the building and you still hear sounds!

The back of the building is perhaps the most frightening. It holds the original hospital kitchen, complete with freezers large enough for storing bodies. It also contains the original operating rooms of the hospital. Abandoned with a sort of reckless carelessness, there are still old X-ray machines, scanning equipment and even rubber tubing hanging from the ceiling, all still somewhat intact (StrangeUSA. com, 2006). It almost feels like a torture room and it leaves the impression that you are in some place which hasn't quite finished being departed. Although they are empty, the six drawers of the morgue in the eastern side of the basement reek of the spirits of the bodies once held there (StrangeUSA.com, 2006).

Any place which has been abandoned, especially over the course of many years of time, has that eerie feeling to it. The mustiness of the air, the dankness of the walls, and the lack of activity combine together to create a sensation which is rarely experienced by people who are busy living within the activity of the every day life. And so, it is to be expected that any exploration into a location which has been abandoned, particularly for a long period of time, is going to stir up the sense that there is something spooky happening around you.

But the Park Presidio's abandoned military hospital has more than just your average sense of spookiness emanating from within. If you stop for a moment within the walls of the building, you can hear that the echoing footsteps continue echoing long after your own feet have stopped moving. If you glance around slowly, you will see that there are patterns of light where there are no windows to let light in. And if you listen closely enough, you might hear the woeful cries of soldiers who tried to be tough while facing the end of their lives, but who can't seem to settle comfortably in to an acceptance of their own deaths.

Crissy Field:
Home For The Lost

Crissy Field is one of those places which had a relatively short period of active life in San Francisco and then kind of disappeared in to the cityscape, only to be rediscovered in recent years and given new life. This seems to be the case with many of the famous locations in San Francisco, due, in part, to the fact that the city is very neighborhood-centric, and money and effort often go into only particular neighborhoods at any given time. As the years pass, renewed interest will generate attention towards a neighborhood which has not been attended to for some time and re-development will take place. These trends are particularly true in areas of the city where the funding for such redevelopment must come directly from the government, as was the case with Crissy Field.

Today, Crissy Field is a 100-acre National Landmark located within the Park Presidio and the Golden Gate National Recreation Area, offering a place of beautiful respite for joggers, bicyclists, and tourists making their way along the water to the Golden Gate Bridge (Crissy Field Center, 2006). However, it took a long time for Crissy Field to get to this point of preservation in its history, a history which has been well-documented by those who have researched the area. The human history of this region of land actually dates back nearly five thousand years when it is believed that persons of Native American descent used the area as a location from which to fish off the shore (Crissy Field Center, 2006).

The more modern history of Crissy Field began during the time of the American Revolution, long before the area was even looking to be considered to be a part of the United States. In that fateful year of 1776, when the bombs were bursting on the East Coast in rejoice over the development of independence by the colonies, the West Coast was being explored by Spanish settlers. They arrived in the San Francisco area and set up the Presidio (Crissy Field Center, 2006). This region of the country was unknown to those who were reveling in the new American culture, and the history of the area is one in which the Spanish settlers nearly eradicated the Native American population to the near-total ignorance of the newly- arrived American people.

In 1821, the country of Mexico gained its independence from the country of Spain and, due to the close proximity and the boundaries of control established by the wars leading up to that independence, the presidio located on the site of what was eventually to become Crissy Field then came under the control of Mexico (Crissy Field Center, 2006). This was not an area of large development for the Mexican government at the time, and things were mostly quiet in the area.

However, in the middle of the nineteenth century, two important national events occurred that greatly affected the development of San Francisco and the history of the Crissy Field region. First, there was the Bear Flag Revolt of 1846, through which Mexico lost control of the Presidio to the American people (Crissy Field Center, 2006). And then there was the Gold Rush, which brought frontiersmen and fortune seekers flooding into the area.

The people of a country, and particularly those people who lead the country either through government control or through access to large portions of wealth, will typically work to defend the wealth of the country. With the gold rush, the wealth of the time was largely concentrated in California, and so there was the sense that the area needed to be protected from outsiders in order to preserve this wealth. In 1855, the construction of Fort Point began in order to aid in this protection of the area (Crissy Field Center, 2006).

The Gold Rush brought people of all natures to the area which is now San Francisco. Life was vibrant and exciting. And this vibrancy continued into the twentieth (and arguably the twenty first) century. In the early twentieth century, much attention of the times was, of course, focused on World War I, and subsequently on the rejuvenation of life after the war. And so, the Presidio area gave way to what became known as Crissy Field, beginning with the development of its army air field (Crissy Field Center, 2006).

The year was 1919. The leading developer of the area was Major Henry H. "Hap" Arnold who discovered the area which would eventually become Crissy Field. Previously used as a race track, the area was claimed by Hap for the army's use (Crissy Field Center, 2006). There was much excitement in the air in those days. World War I was over, the economy was rising, and people were interested in celebrating.

One of the ways in which the army was celebrating was through the development of air shows. Crissy Field seemed to be a perfect place to highlight the skills of army pilots, and before the area was even fully developed, a San Francisco team, led by Major Dana H. Crissy, began to participate in public air displays. These new events were extremely popular during this time, with the concept of humans flying through the air being brand-new and filling people across the world with a sense of the accomplishments which can be achieved by the untamed human spirit. The air shows gave American people a chance to celebrate their strengths and ingenuity, and this was a time during which people gathered together in laughter and optimism.

Unfortunately, all was not fun and games. Major Crissy was one of many men who participated in these events, and his participation offered him both lifelong glory and an untimely demise. In October 1919, Major Crissy was one of sixty-one men who engaged in a test of human flight endurance (Styles, 2002). The army-hosted event, called the First Transcontinental Reliability and Endurance Test, pitted forty-six pilots on the East Coast against fifteen pilots on the West Coast in a competition to see which pilot could fly across the entire country and land on the opposite coast first (Styles, 2002).

Major Crissy must have left the West Coast filled with excitement and hope that he might be one of what turned out to only be nine men to complete this amazing task (Styles, 2002). But Major Crissy would never see the East Coast. An emergency occurred just over Salt Lake City, resulting in a crash landing which caused the death of the young Major. His observer, Sgt. 1st Class V. Thomas, was also killed in the landing (Styles, 2002).

Crissy Field continued to be developed in spite of this tragedy with which it was sadly associated. In honor of the man who had lost his life trying to further the limits of flight exploration and inspire the American people, Hap opted to name the newly-completed air field after Major Crissy (Styles, 2002). And in spite of this tragic event, the area continued to grow. Money continued to flow through the United States economy for a short period of time, and in 1920, the government approved one million dollars for use in expanding Crissy Field. Developments included improved air fields, the installation of canons, and the construction of numerous buildings and barracks (Crissy Field Center, 2006).

Crissy Field was a lively place for approximately another decade, but then the wear and tear to the air field, along with the new development (and resulting traffic) of the Golden Gate Bridge, began to make Crissy Field less and less appealing for regular use by the American military. It was not long before the area was abandoned. There was a brief period of re-use of the area during World War II, but for many years before and after that time, the area was mostly untouched.

Of course, when living people move out of an area, spirits sometimes move in. This is believed by many to be what happened with Crissy Field. Some say it is the ghost of Major Crissy coming back to regain some of his dignity. Others say that they believe the disruption of the calm Native American way of life by the Spanish settlers so many years ago gave Native spirits a reason to make this their resting place. Still others say that the spirits of the Crissy Field area are those who could find no other place to settle in the city and so moved out to the abandoned location where they could continue their days in relative peace.

Today, these spirits co-exist with the living. Crissy Field has been renovated to become a public beach and historic museum highlighting the interesting aeronautical history of the once-populated army base. The transformation was slow in coming, but has achieved outstanding results. In 1972, the Golden Gate National Recreation Area was established in the region surrounding Crissy Field (Crissy Field Center, 2006). Almost twenty years later, the military officially gave over control of Crissy Field to the National Park Service for inclusion in this recreation area (Crissy Field Center, 2006).

In 1998, work began to re-develop what was then the overgrown air field, which was covered in rotting vegetation mingled with the massive untouched asphalt of the air field days (NPCA, 2006). It took three years before the area was open to the public, but once it was, the people of San Francisco were graced with a new beautiful urban retreat featuring twenty acres of tidal marsh, nearly thirty acres of grassy area, and walking and bicycle paths (NPCA, 2006). Travelers can take a walk from the field to Fort Point, passing through the old canon cells which still remain there.

However, you may find that if you are walking in the area on a lonely day, when tourist traffic is low and the number of people in the area is few, that there are more spirits in this section of the city than you might find that you are comfortable being around. Perhaps you will hear that drumming of a Native American tribal band. Or maybe you will hear the roar of an airplane engine without seeing one appear in the sky. Pay close attention when walking through this glorious urban park area; you might think that you can feel the chilly wind that you hear whipping through the canons ... that is, until you realize that there is no wind in the air, and that the chill is going directly to your bones.

Haskell House:
A Slice Of Old West History

The story of the Haskell House is straight out of the history of the Old West which marks the early development of San Francisco. During that era, in the middle of the nineteenth century, rugged frontiersmen and political leaders were one and the same, and they often settled their disputes in rough and violent ways which would never be tolerated today. Such was the case between United States Senator David Broderick and State Supreme Court Justice David Terry.

It was 1857, and the big question on everyone's agenda was the issue of slavery (GAzis-SAx, 1996). Should slavery be allowed? Should it be up to the states as to whether or not it was allowed? Who, in this young country, was going to be able to make these decisions? When the question came to California, Broderick and Terry found that they were on opposite sides of the heated debate. Broderick believed that California should be free of slavery while Terry felt that slavery was necessary to the economic development of the state (Hauck, 2006). The two were embroiled in ongoing argument over the issue which grew until it included personal verbal attacks on one another, in which they challenged each other to stand up to the words they each issued against their enemy (GAzis-SAx, 1996).

In today's world, this type of issue would be debated endlessly; people would choose positions, and votes and political tools would be employed to make a decision. In today's world, the decision would not even necessarily be a lasting one, as we have grown enough as a country to see the way in which the winds change as new information and new experiences in our society shift things for us. But Broderick and Terry did not live in today's world. They lived in an era during which every decision seemed to be imminently important, as it was shaping the future of this country. And they lived in an era when debates were not always settled with words.

Broderick and Terry agreed to engage in a gun duel. It was Terry who challenged the duel, and Broderick was a true man of his times, unable to back down from the challenge lest he be seen as a coward (GAzis-SAx, 1996). The two men met, exchanged insults and tried to sway each other to their own side of the opinionated issue. In the end, they faced each other. It was straight out of a Western movie; the two stood apart, their hands at their holsters, ready to draw their guns at the appointed time. Whoever was left standing would win the argument for the State of California.

However, things went awry. Broderick's hand on his holster slipped and he hadn't even removed it when the gun went off (GAzis-SAx, 1996). In automatic reaction, Terry pulled his own gun and shot in Broderick's direction (GAzis-SAx, 1996). Broderick was struck. He lived for a few hours, making his way to the home of Leonides Haskell, located at the end of Franklin Street in Quarters Three of Fort Mason fort, where he eventually died from the bullet wound (GAzis-SAx, 1996).

As justice would have it, despite his untimely demise, Broderick won the debate. Terry's desire to see slavery thrive in California was circumvented by the outcome of the civil war and the changing of the political tides. However, Broderick doesn't seem to be satisfied with the solution to the problem of slavery, or perhaps he just wants to let everyone know that he won in spite of not being around in person to see it, because he hasn't left the Haskell House since the day that he died.

Numerous army officials have been housed at Fort Mason over the years, but not too many of them stay long, and the history of hauntings in the house has been so prevalent that the United States government actually engages in the unusual practice of telling its officers about the hauntings prior to their move-in date so that they can prepare themselves (Hauck, 2006).

Colonel Cecil Puckett was one of the officers who lived in the home and who experienced the ghost of David Broderick (Hauck, 2006). He lived there throughout much of the 1970s, and although he was never particularly bothered by the ghost, few days would pass when he didn't feel the presence of the man following him throughout the house. Puckett says that Broderick spends most of his time in the kitchen, although he would also frequently watch Puckett shower (Hauck, 2006). For some reason, Broderick must like the bathrooms and eating areas of the home, because Captain Jim Knight reported that during the two years that he lived there, the dining room lights would frequently turn off and on "by themselves" and the toilet would flush without assistance from anyone that Knight could see (Hauck, 2006).

Because of the frequency of such reports, and the government's warning to occupants of the Haskell House, the tough military men who live there sometimes take to joking about the spirits as a means of handling the discomfort of the spooky situation. Captain Everett Jones was one such officer. He lived in the Haskell House for over three years, and when he first moved in, he was a non-believer but by the time that he left, he was certain that the home was haunted (Hauck, 2006). In the beginning, he and his family would joke about the presence of ghosts. But when fixtures began falling, pictures began crashing to the floor and chills began spreading through the home, Jones stopped joking. Once the jokes stopped, the more disastrous activity stopped as well, although the presence of spirits could be felt throughout the home during the time that Jones lived there.

Captain James Lunn is perhaps the most recent occupant of the Haskell Home to report spirits. He and his family have seen shadows moving through the parlor of the house. Plants fall over, the ears of the family's dog prick to no apparent sound, and there is an overall sensation that the house is occupied. During construction, a painter was pushed out of a window and he swears to this day that there was no one in the room with him when he felt himself pushed to fall (GAzis-SAx, 1996).

Because the hauntings seemed to be increasing for a time, psychic Sylvia Brown was called in to assess the situation. During her stay in the home, she saw a number of different spirits, including a man in a long black coat and top hat tapping at the window, a man which has been seen by numerous guests of the location over time (GAzis-SAx, 1996). Interestingly, Browne also saw that there were a number of African American people hiding in the cellar of the Haskell House. She believes that they were there for their own protection, although they were ultimately unhappy with their hidden state (GAzis-SAx, 1996).

Although San Francisco's history has been recorded by many, there are undoubtedly pieces of it which aren't yet known. It makes one wonder what relationship Broderick, supporter of a free state, had with the Haskell Home where his life came to an end. There is no record of the home being used as a refuge or hiding place by Bay Area African Americans, but a lack of recorded history does not mean a lack of experience.

Visitors interested in exploring the history of the area do not need to work too hard to do so. The Haskell House is no longer a private residence but instead is a part of the Golden Gate National Recreation Area which preserves the military history of the area that once thrived there (GAzis-SAx, 1996). The site of the duel between Terry and Broderick can be visited by San Francisco guests who can even stand in the exact locations of the opponents which are marked out for tourists (GAzis-SAx, 1996). And for those who are open to the idea, Broderick's ghost reportedly still lingers around, watching over the events of history as they unfold.

Part IV:
Schools

Perhaps one of the most uncomfortable places to experience the presence of a spirit is within the halls of a school. Educational institutions, like people's homes, are intended to be safe havens. Although this is obviously not always the case, it is at least the hope of parents sending their children off to school. Nonetheless, tragedy does occur in classrooms and when it does, the spirits of those affected by it may have trouble moving on.

Whether it is within the child-sized bathrooms of elementary schools or the housing of college dorms, spirits in such places are particularly spooky. They may not be any more bothersome than ghosts in other locations, but there is just something about a spirit that wants to spend eternity lingering in the halls of a school which is more than a little bit unsettling.

CCS Elementary School:
An Old Woman's Return To Youth

If you enter the halls of CCS Elementary School during the daylight hours, you are likely to hear the excited laughter of children roaming throughout the building. Giggling in lines as their teachers try to get them organized for lunch, reading aloud as part of their daily lesson plans, and screaming in fun while playing games during recess, the children of CCS are like children at any other elementary school in the country, children with hardly a care in the world.

Chinese Christian Schools says on its website that "our school cannot be understood just by reading—you have to visit to sense the vitality, energy, and spirit of our school community" (Chinese Christian Schools, 2006). CCS certainly provides an interesting education for its students. The school emphasizes not only academics, but a combination of Christian philosophy and Chinese culture, creating a student body which is diverse and well-educated in both the eastern and western worlds (Chinese Christian Schools, 2006). But what they don't advertise on their website is the fact that perhaps there is more than just the energy of creative instructors and excited children pulsating through the halls of CCS.

If you enter the halls of CCS Elementary School during the hours when class is not in session, the sounds you hear will not be the sounds of laughing youth, and the screams coming from the playground might be those flying out of your own throat as you make your way out of the haunted building as fast as you possibly can.

This is because CCS Elementary School is said to be haunted by the ghost of an elderly woman who was murdered in the building (S.F. Heart, 2006). It may be just an urban legend, but it is said that she was pushed down a staircase, where she lay in a heap until her murderer picked up her lifeless body and placed it in the dumpster out back (S.F. Hearts, 2006).

It is not known why this woman chooses to remain in the place of her untimely death. Perhaps she is still seeking justice for the murderers who were never caught, or maybe she just isn't quite sure how to move on. But whatever the reason, she has stayed in the school. When the games of the children go quiet, you can hear her praying Hail Mary in the girls' bathroom located by the staircase (StrangeUSA.com, 2006).

Abraham Lincoln and Washington High Schools

High school can be a frightening place for many teenagers. The taunts, the teasing, the pressure of trying to do well enough to get into a good college but still fit into the social world that is ever-so-critical at that stage of life … it can all be overwhelming. But there is more than just the typical high school problems to be afraid of at both Abraham Lincoln High School and Washington High School.

Whereas most kids want to get out of high school as quickly as possible, not all youth who have passed through these hallways seem to be as eager to leave these schools as rapidly as one would think. In fact, there seems to be more than one spirit lingering in the halls and walls of these two San Francisco educational spots.

Abraham Lincoln High School

The girls' bathrooms seem to be where the spirits tend to linger, indicating that there's either a girl who doesn't want to give up the best four years of her life or there's a boy who is trying to see more than he could when he attended the school. The spirits are found in both the bathroom located near the main office of the school, as well as the bathroom located by the band room, although it is uncertain whether it is the same or different spirits lingering in these two locations (S.F. Heart, 2006).

The bathroom by the main office is relatively quiet. However, on more than one occasion, the first person to enter the bathroom in the morning will find that all of the toilet paper has been unraveled on to the floor. (S.F. Heart, 2006). It could be a case of vandalism, except that it has happened regularly, without any other signs of break-in or damage, and it has always happened at night when no one could enter the locked building without being noticed (S.F. Heart, 2006).

The bathroom by the band room is not nearly so quiet. The spirit there seems to want to communicate with people as they enter the room, although he or she is shy to do so, only lightly whispering "hello" on rare occasions (S.F. Heart, 2006). Numerous girls have reported peeking underneath stall doors to check if anyone is in the stall and seeing feet there, only to find that nobody is actually in the stall.

Washington High School

In Washington High School, it is the boys' bathroom which seems to be the spot where someone simply can't stand the thought of leaving (S.F. Heart, 2006). The male bathroom on the third floor bustles with activity during the day, as kids stop in between classes to take care of their private business. But at night, security staff and teachers who have had to stay late to grade papers or safely walk the halls have reported seeing a figure standing near one of the stalls in this bathroom. The figure is usually seen out of the corner of an eye and dissipates when the viewer tries to get a grasp on what is going on. No one knows who this spirit is.

San Francisco Art Institute:
The Art World Accepts Unusual Activity

San Francisco is a place where creative people have always thrived. The Beat Poets of North Beach are just one example from the past (and the muralists of the Mission just one example from the present) of individual artists who came together in San Francisco at a single point in time to create a scene that helps to define an entire generation. There is vibrancy everywhere one turns in the city. Interest in art here takes many forms, perhaps one of the most formal of which is the prevalence of art education options in the city.

The San Francisco Art Institute (SFAI) is one of those institutions of education in art of all kinds. It is considered, by many, to be the most prestigious of art schools located in the Bay Area, due at least in part, to the fact that it has been in existence since 1871 (SFAI, 2006). This long history alone is enough to suggest that spirits may be present in the location. It is no secret that many artists are tortured souls, at least for some time during their lives. It is also no secret that artists tend to have a higher proclivity for being tuned into the spirit world and the questioning of reality than does the average person. So, it is no surprise then that spirits are known for haunting the buildings of SFAI and that people there frequently accept with little question that this is something which occurs.

The main campus of the art institute is located at 800 Chestnut Street, between the North Beach and Russian Hill neighborhoods of San Francisco, in a location which was once a monastery and once a cemetery (Foreman, 1999). If these two types of history are not enough to create the setting for a spirit to linger, their combination with the creative distress of the art world seems to be the necessary component, because this place has been haunted for as long as students have been attending the school.

Numerous different sightings of spirits have happened at SFAI over the years (Hauck, 2006). The most common location for such experiences to occur is the watch tower which is part of the original construction of the monastery (Foreman, 1999). The tower has been haunted for more than half a century. It was opened in 1927, and from day one people began commenting that there was a strange feeling in the air up in that tower (Richards, 2004).

One of the first recognized reports of spirit presence in the SFAI tower was by Bill Morehouse, a former student of the arts there (Richards, 2004). The first time that he reported experiencing something unusual, he had been watching the tower's third level from the inside. He heard footsteps coming up the stairs. He called out to see who was coming but no response came. The door opened and closed behind a presence, but there was no one there. The presence proceeded to walk, with audible footsteps, past Morehouse to the tower's observation deck (Foreman, 1999).

Morehouse reported this experience to friends who didn't believe that he was telling the truth. Then, a group of them gathered together in the tower one night to have a surprise party for a friend. They were all waiting in the tower room for the friend to arrive when they heard what they thought was the friend's footsteps on the stairs. They opened the door to yell "surprise"—but to *their* surprise, no one was there (Richards, 2004).

Morehouse is not the only one who has had these experiences. Wally Hedrick, who once worked at SFAI, reported hearing all of the tools in the sculpture studio begin working at once, although no one was in the studio at the time (Richards, 2004). Hayward King worked at the location at the same time as Wally Hedrick and would experience something similar; at the end of his shift, he would turn off all of the lights in the building, but when he'd get back downstairs, he could see that some of them had turned back on. On one occasion, Hedrick and King were working together, and they made the usual rounds, turning off all of the lights. They exited the building and just as the door closed shut behind them, all of the lights in the building simultaneously turned on (Richards, 2004).

For awhile, after the experiences of these three men, the SFAI tower was quiet — or at least no one was reporting any problems. But the spirits hadn't left the building. Perhaps they had just become comfortable with the way that things were there and didn't need to bother anyone. In 1968, renovation on the SFAI tower began (Richards, 2004). The spirits did not like their peaceful existence disturbed. Immediately, a number of strange and tragic events began to take place.

During the renovation itself, three different near-tragedies took place (Hauck, 2006). It was not only the shared experiences of these people which indicated that something was amiss. Spirits made themselves known all throughout the tower. The sounds of destruction which echoed throughout the building often came when work on the tower was not taking place. Chairs would be heard splintering in to pieces, with no one there to cause the damage, and unidentifiable shrieks were common (Richards, 2004).

In years since, séances have been held and groups of psychics have spent time in the SFAI tower trying to figure out who was haunting the area. Some of the most famous names in Bay Area ghostly experiences have checked out the place. Nick Nocerino came in and took photographs of the tower room, which showed the tower to be exactly as it was at the time the photos were taken—except that there were doors and a window in the photo which were not in the same place in the room, indicating that Nocerino was able to capture pictures of the tower from a time before the renovations (Richards, 2004). Chuck Pelton is another photographer who has captured photos of things appearing from how they are to the naked eye. His photographs of the SFAI tower show displaced people all throughout the room (Richards, 2004).

There is much debate as to who the spirits are that haunt this tower. A general séance once found "frustrated spirits" in the location (Richards, 2004). A more specific exploration by Antoinette May found that the spirits were those of artists who failed to realize their creativity in life and so needed attention in death (Richards, 2004). In contrast, an in-depth exploration by San Jose medium Amy Chandler ended with her determination that there was a lost graveyard beneath the building—a fact which she didn't know prior to entering the building but later, through research, proved to be true (Richards, 2004).

The art world is a complex place. It is filled with hope and inspiration and creativity which know few bounds. It is also filled with terror and despair and the inner struggle of people who often feel as if they do not quite belong in this world. This combination creates a dynamic setting in which spirits may get trapped. In turn, the spirit world provides great fodder for the artistic imagination. No one can say for sure what is happening in the SFAI tower right now, but even those with creative minds may find that the reality is more than they could handle.

Part V:

Miscellaneous Locations

Of course, tragedies can happen in any place. Spirits may linger in the strangest of locations, sometimes because they have an association with the place during their lives and sometimes because the place is linked to them in their deaths. Cemeteries are moved and once-settled spirits are freed and left to wander. Accidents happen and souls get stuck where they have died. San Francisco, with its rich history, is a location where a spirit may be found around nearly any corner.

Bay Bridge:
Earthquake's Lonesome Tragedy

It was October 17th, 1989. Game 3 of the World Series. All of the Bay Area's eyes were turned to baseball because the two local teams were pitted against each other. Before the game even began, the rivalry between San Francisco proper and the East Bay was going strong with the former waving orange and black flags in honor of their San Francisco Giants and the latter holding up their A's penants in support of the Oakland Athletics (Wikipedia, 2006).

Sports journalists all over the area were getting in their stories and making their predictions. Kevin Cowherd zipped through his article for the *The Baltimore Sun* in time for it to be reprinted in *The San Jose Mercury News* on the morning of the event. In his column, he noted the struggle between the two local teams in Game 3 and added, "God only knows if they'll even get all the games in. An earthquake could rip through the Bay Area before they sing the national anthem" (Wikipedia, 2006).

The game hadn't started. The national anthem had not yet been sung. Loma Prieta Earthquake hit. Though it would eventually become well-known as a local tragedy, the Loma Prieta earthquake is not the one most people think of when they think of historical earthquakes in San Francisco. Instead, it is the 1906 earthquake which comes to everyone's minds. But the two are inextricably linked. The 1906 earthquake destroyed much of the area on the edge of the bay. Without anywhere to put the mess, city crews bulldozed much of the city's remains into the bay (Wikipedia, 2006).

Because much of the land beneath the bay water consisted of this mess, it was highly unstable. Buildings built all over this land were ruined in the1989 earthquake. And buildings were not the only thing to go down when Loma Prieta hit. Interstate 80 trembled in the wake of the earthquake, and the two-tier San Francisco-Oakland Bay Bridge shuddered in response. A small section of the top deck collapsed. It was only fifty feet in length, but it caused two cars to fall onto the bottom deck (Wikipedia, 2006).

As far as disasters go, this one could have been much worse. The fact that Game 3 was about to begin worked in the favor of the residents of the area. Normal commuter traffic on the Bay Bridge was at a low because so much of the city had gotten out of work early to attend to the game. Many of the area's residents were already at Candlestick Park, waiting for the game to begin, far away from the damage where the earthquake hit hardest (Wikipedia, 2006).

But that was not the case for one lone man. When that small section of the bridge collapsed and the two cars fell, he was killed. A single fatality on that stretch of space. And some say that he has remained trapped there ever since.

The damage from the Loma Prieta Earthquake has all been repaired. But if you drive across the bridge, headed along the lower deck towards Oakland, you just might hear a light tap on your car window. It sounds almost like the crack of a baseball bat making contact with a ball. And if you glance over to find the source of the sound, you might see a headless man running next to your car, keeping pace with you. But don't worry, when you reach the end of the bridge, he will disappear back in to the bay (S.F. Heart, 2006). He apparently doesn't want to leave the site of his life's unexpected ending.

California Street:
A Girl Returns Home

There are some ghosts that are only experienced directly by one living person, usually in the case of a spirit trying to get a message to their still-living loved one. And then there are some ghosts which make enough of a splash in the scene of the living that there are people from across place and time who report seeing the spirit. Flora Summerton is one of those ghosts. In fact, she is the ghost who is said to be the single most reported ghost sighting in all of San Francisco (Graf, 2006).

There are numerous interesting stories related to the sightings of her as a ghost, but it is the story of Flora's life which makes an interesting beginning to the fascinating tale of her first sighting in the city. This is because Flora's life was both romantic and tragic, real and yet surreal, and it is precisely this kind of life which is most likely to lead to continued presence on earth after death—or at least to belief by others that a character like Flora Summerton might want to stick around.

The year was 1876. Flora was a beautiful young woman who lived in a glorious home on California Street in the Nob Hill neighborhood of San Francisco. Everything about Flora's life looked perfect from the outside. She was a stunning girl from a prestigious family, living in an exclusive area and looking forward to a fantastic future with a handsome groom. Beautiful is all well and good, but it has never been known to make a person truly happy, and Flora suffered from problems with a gripping depression throughout her life, problems which her access to money and material beauty could not defy. In later adolescence, this depression was exacerbated in large part by the fact that, at just eighteen years of age, she was being married off to a man that she did not want to marry by parents who thought that they knew what was best for her (Graf, 2006).

Flora's parents went all out with the planning and execution of her engagement party, inviting all of the socially acceptable people that they knew to partake in their enjoyment of this theoretically delightful event. It was a time and place when only the most appropriate behavior was to be displayed in public. Flora tried to play the part well. She dressed up in a flowing gown decorated with elaborate beadwork and got dolled up to welcome her guests (Graf, 2006).

Then she panicked. Just before the engagement was to be announced, she fled from the home in terror. She ran up California Street, over one of the steepest hills in San Francisco and disappeared, never to be heard from again (Graf, 2006). Almost. Her parents searched for her, expending the bulk of their resources in an attempt to figure out where the girl had gone (Graf, 2006). Her bewildered groom also made efforts to locate the girl. But for as long as they were looking, Flora remained nothing but a ghost in their memories.

And then, years later, Flora returned. In 1926, far away from San Francisco in the town of Butte, Montana, the body of a 68-year-old woman was discovered in a boarding house, a body which turned out to belong to Ms. Flora Summerton (Graf, 2006). The body was swathed with the fabric of her beautiful wedding dress, and suddenly the few people who were still around to remember that fateful day when Flora ran away had an inkling of knowledge about where she had gone (Graf, 2006).

The day that the woman's body was discovered in Montana, the ghost of Flora Summerton was sighted for the first time in San Francisco. She was in tears, her face a beautiful anguished mess, her dress on the verge of tearing as she ran up California Street (Graf, 2006). Flora may have escaped the fate of marrying a man that she didn't want to marry, but she clearly didn't make peace within her Montana-spent adulthood because she now haunts the scene of her San Francisco farewell. Her spirit has been sighted by numerous locals and travelers, including those who have participated in the ghost hunt tours which travel on foot through the area (Graf, 2006).

Curran Theatre:
Murder Captures Man In Time

The sad truth about most ghost stories is that they mostly start with sad tales. As a result of the fact that death came quickly and untimely for certain people, there is a tendency for those spirits to linger, trying to resolve the unresolved issues of the past before being able to move on to their own futures in a more timeless world. Tragedy is the case of the most famous ghost of the Curran Theatre, although this is not the only ghost who haunts the location. In fact, this haunted spot has been reported to have nearly 300 ghosts wandering around its interior, the stories of whom are mostly untold.

But it is the death of Hewlett Tarr which is the tragedy that seemed to start the history of the hauntings of this famous San Francisco theatre. It was the early 1930s, a spirited time during which attending the theatre was a popular way of passing the hours. Hewlett Tarr was gainfully employed as a ticket taker for the Curran Theatre, working to have money in order to go out and have fun with his fiancé and the other young people who populated his social world.

But times were not prosperous for everyone. Eddie Anderson was one such person who lacked the funds necessary to enjoy the San Francisco nightlife to the degree which he desired. More specifically, Eddie Anderson had a girlfriend who wanted to enjoy that nightlife and Eddie would do anything to please that girl (May, 2004). In desperation, Eddie entered a life of petty crime.

One fateful night, the lives of Hewlett Tarr and Eddie Anderson merged. Anderson's girlfriend wanted to attend the theatre like the other fancy folk in town. Anderson wanted to make his girlfriend happy. He made his way to the Curran Theatre intending to get the tickets to please the girl. Hewlett Tarr was working the ticket counter that night, selling tickets to *Show Boat*, when Eddie arrived, pulled out his gun and demanded that Hewlett give him two tickets to that night's show (Collins, 2003).

According to the story as told by Eddie at the time, he never intended to shoot Hewlett. This is probably true, since Eddie's previous crimes had been non-violent. However, the theater ticket robbery went awry. Eddie had pressed the gun between the rails at the ticket office window and it had gotten caught there and fired. Hewlett was directly hit. He fell backwards, his body growing limp as it cascaded down the flight of stairs behind him. That was where Hewlett Tarr's life would end, in a crumpled heap at the bottom of the Curran Theater's stairwell. But that is not the end of Hewlett's story (May, 2004).

Eddie Anderson panicked and ran from the theater. He went on a brief spree of petty crime, robbing the nearby Koffe Kup restaurant almost immediately and proceeding to rob a bank a short time later (Collins, 2003). He was caught two weeks after the shooting of Hewlett Tarr by police and a trial ensued. Hewlett's fiancée, Dorothy Reed, appeared daily at the trial, hoping for some relief from her grief and some vindication for her pain. The jury saw things her way and Anderson was convicted and sentenced to death. He served time at San Quentin State Penitentiary where he was hanged and buried. That was the end of Eddie's story (May, 2004).

However, the effect he had on this world lingers on long past the years that he spent living it, because Hewlett Tarr appears to have never gained enough peace to move on after the shooting death caused by Eddie Anderson. Tarr's spirit remains stuck at the Curran Theatre. The theatre, that today shows primarily Broadway shows and musicals, is located at 445 Geary Street. Walking into the entry way of the theatre, you will notice a large mirror, and if Hewlett is hanging around at the time, you will see his reflection in place of yours (May, 2004). Dressed in the style of the 1930s, the handsome man will eye you with a bewildered look in his eye, as though he is still trying to figure out why he was shot.

Dolores Park:
Movement Unsettles The Dead

The world of spirits is a murky one, and it is often hard to separate the history from the legend, the truth from the fiction, the concrete from the mystical. This feat is complicated further in situations where a location seems to be haunted by multiple spirits. It becomes almost impossible when the presence of the spirits seem to follow certain people from one location to another. To understand such a situation, you have to be willing to accept that sometimes things are not as clear as we would like them to be in the telling of our stories. Ghosts do not live in the sort of timeline in which we live our daily lives, and they do not move through space in the same tangible way in which we do. To understand their presence in an area, we have to suspend our way of thinking for awhile and accept that maybe things do not have to be entirely clear in order to be understood.

This is the case with Dolores Park. The history of the area is too complicated to understand with simple ease. The presence of two different cemeteries on the site at different times makes it hard to discern when spirits began appearing at the haunted location. The fact that certain people seem to have experienced the same spirits both at Dolores Park and elsewhere makes Dolores Park that much more difficult to understand. But whether or not we understand it, it is clear that something a bit unreal is happening in that area of San Francisco.

The story of Dolores Park is one of those stories which is best not told in linear fashion. Things do not proceed cleanly from "this happened" to "that happened" in the history of Dolores Park and the spirits who linger—or filter through—there. Instead, the story of Dolores Park is one in which multiple characters weave back and forth through time.

So the story begins with modern times and a young woman named Collette Brumfield (Spataro, 1999). Collette experienced her first encounter with the spirit world one day when she was spending time with her boyfriend, John, enjoying the peaceful beauty of Dolores Park. The two of them were the only ones in the park at the time, and they were engaged in laughing conversation on one of the park benches, immersed in the world between them and nearly oblivious to the world around them, when, suddenly, they both heard the sound of someone clapping (Spataro, 1999).

They looked around, but saw no one, and they couldn't quite tell where the source of the sound was emanating from. After spending some time listening to the otherworldly clapping, they determined that it sounded as though the clapping was coming from behind a nearby tree, but when John went to see if anyone was there, no one could be found (Spataro, 1999). As John moved around the park in search of the maker of the sound, he and Collette began to hear laughter. Each of them felt the presence of other people in the park, but they could see through the open space of the urban retreat and no one else appeared to be there. The experience spooked Collette so intensely that they left the park immediately and both waited quite some time before ever returning (Spataro, 1999).

If this was all that there was to the history of hauntings in Dolores Park, it could be passed off as an isolated incident which may not be indicative of ghost activity at all. It could be assumed that somebody was playing a prank on the young couple and just had the lighting and the atmosphere right enough to pull it off. But the Dolores Park experience was not the only experience that Collette's boyfriend, John, would have with a ghost.

For a time, John lived in a home in the Pacific Heights neighborhood of San Francisco. There was no doubt in his mind that a spirit was haunting the location. Doors would close without assistance, lights would flicker regularly. The presence of spirits became so disarming that eventually a priest was called to the house to discern what was going on and (hopefully) to expel the spirits from the location. During the priest's visit, lights in the home flickered uncontrollably, doors slammed, and there was suddenly an animalistic roar emanating from downstairs (Spataro, 1999).

John's experience in the Pacific Heights home could be considered unrelated to his experience in Dolores Park that day that he and Collette were together. However, history begs to differ. John's Pacific Heights home was built atop the original location of a Hebrew Cemetery. As San Francisco grew, the Hebrew Cemetery was dug up and moved ... directly to the location which would eventually become Dolores Park!

The Hebrew Cemetery was closed in 1860, shortly after it was moved to Dolores Park. The following year, a new Jewish Cemetery, the Gibbath Olum Cemetery, opened in the same location (bordered by Church Street, Dolores, 18th and 20th). The Gibbath Olum Cemetery remained open until 1888, at which time the settled bodies were again shifted, this time to nearby Colma (Spataro, 1999). Perhaps all of this shifting is what has made it so difficult for the people once buried in the area to know where to spend the rest of their days and nights.

Neptune Society Columbarium:
Unburied Stories

Today, the Richmond neighborhood of San Francisco is a combination of shopping, dining, nightlife, and residences. Located close to the popular beaches of Ocean Beach and Baker Beach, the Richmond is visited by tourists and locals alike. Shrouded in fog even on the warmest of San Francisco days, this area may buzz with activity, but the hum underneath the active life taking place there is one which comes from another world.

This area of San Francisco was one of the last places to be developed within the city limits. Originally, it was all sand dunes leading up to the beach. When the city began to make use of the area, it was to build cemeteries. Four cemeteries covering more than one hundred and fifty acres of land in the Richmond district were home to the remains of a diverse group of people.

The cemeteries no longer remain, having been moved to Colma relatively early in the twentieth century. However, there is a physical memory of this part of the city's past located at 1 Loraine Court (near the intersection of Geary and Stanyan). The old crematorium, which was abandoned throughout a large portion of the mid-twentieth century, was taken over by the Neptune Society in 1979, to be used as a public landmark.

The building itself is visited for a number of reasons, including the stained glass architecture and artifacts which are housed there today. People from all over the world who have an interest in San Francisco architecture may visit the area. However, art is not all that is held at this location.

During a trip to the landmark, one visitor felt a hand pressed against her back. She turned around to find that no one was near her. Those with her eyed the back of her shirt warily, as there was a thin white handprint marking the spot where she felt that she had been touched (S.F. Heart, 2006). There is lasting value in the artifacts available for view at the Neptune Society Columbarium, but perhaps some of those who were uprooted from the area think that their personal tales are a little bit more valuable.

Golden Gate Park:
Large Enough for Loads of Spirits

Golden Gate Park is an immense haven of peaceful nature inside the urban world of San Francisco. The park extends through the city for the length of over forty avenues, offering San Franciscans a place to enjoy the year-round moderate temperatures of the Bay Area. Within the boundaries of the park, travelers and locals alike can enjoy the tea-sipping serenity of the Japanese Tea Gardens, the lush vegetation of the Botanical Gardens, the viewing of American Bison, the cherry blossoms falling seasonally from the trees, modern museums, plays in the park, and recreational activities. It would take weeks of endless exploration to enjoy every crevice of this amazing place.

But not all is quiet and peaceful in Golden Gate Park. Its long history has led to moments in time when what took place in the park was less than pleasant, and the people whose lives were linked to those personal disasters linger in the peace of the pleasant park, reminding those taking pleasure in the place today that all history includes harsh history.

Strawberry Hill is one location in Golden Gate Park where those who don't wish to encounter spirits should avoid spending time. It is located at Stowe Lake, a place where people go to enjoy a beautiful day in the park. Paddle boats can be rented at this largest of the park's nine lakes, and many people take the boats to the man-made island of Strawberry Hill to enjoy picnicking or frolicking. The lake has been a part of the park since before the turn of the twentieth century, and many people have wonderful memories associated with days spent there.

But in the 1920s, one woman used Stowe Lake as a place to create memories from which she still can not escape. She was young, and she was pregnant, and she wasn't sure what she was going to do in this era when it was not appropriate to be unwed and with child. She hid the pregnancy and had the baby, but she had not yet figured out how she was going to raise the child. In desperation, she made her way to Stowe Lake, late at night, to spend some time thinking over what she was going to do.

As she mulled over her options, they seemed increasingly narrow. She sat at the base of the lake, perhaps dangling her feet in the water and trying to come up with a plan. No plan came to her. Finally, she determined that she could not go on. She disposed of the child and then drowned herself in the lake. It has been over eighty years since that time, but the woman is stuck in her own murky past. She continues to walk around Stowe Lake in search of the child who was never allowed to grow up (S.F. Heart, 2006).

Not all of Golden Gate Park's ghosts are associated with such painful stories. In fact, there is one ghost there who doesn't have a history specifically associated with the park, at least not one which anyone has been able to figure out, and yet he spends time there on a frequent basis. If you ever find yourself driving through the park, you might encounter him, but you may not realize that he's not real at first, because he appears in a very realistic police car complete with sirens and flashing lights.

This Golden Gate Park police officer will exit his car, ticket you (for speeding, usually, although he has issued tickets for slow driving, recklessness, and illegal turns), and you will think that you've merely had bad luck with the law. However, you should contest your ticket, because chances are that the officer is not going to show up at the courthouse. No, he's not just a lazy cop; he's been dead for more than a dozen years.

It is said that if you find yourself getting pulled over in the park, you should drive to the boundaries of the park and watch the officer disappear into the fog behind you (S.F. Heart, 2006). Of course, driving away from an officer is never really recommended, and the cop is friendly to everyone he's pulled over, so you may just want to move your car to the side of the road and live out this ghostly experience.

After all, if you've got a choice between a wounded mother searching for her lost child and a friendly chat with an officer who doesn't exist, which one makes more sense to accept as just one more piece of your life story?

Trinity Episcopal Church:
Spirits In Spirituality

Trinity Episcopal Church stands as an ostentatious historical landmark located at the intersection of Bush Street and Gough. Built in the late nineteenth century, this magnificent building is both a model of architectural style and a place of historical significance, both factors of which are due in part to the fact that the church pre-dates the 1906 earthquake which ravaged the area.

Just looking at the church from the outside, it is obvious that the building is solidly built. Its stone structure is constructed in a manner designed to look like a fortress from the medieval times. The effect is enhanced by the jarring towers and the guarding gargoyles which detail the exterior. It is a structure which hints at haunt from the outside in.

The interior design is not as haunting as the exterior. The raised ceilings and open stained glass windows offer a lightness which relieves some of the intensity of the church's façade. The frightening faces of the outside gargoyles are replaced by the cherubic faces of bronze angels. However, this peacefulness belies an active spirit presence.

There are at least two different spirits which seem to haunt the Trinity Episcopal Church. One is a grayish figure which is frequently seen exiting the men's bathroom within the church. The other is the ghost of a man in a white suit who wanders the pews and startles the visitors who are politely praying. In addition to these specific spirits, the church is haunted by strange shadows and three-directional drafts which do not have a visible source (S.F. Heart, 2006).

No harm has come to anyone sighting spirits in this place of worship, but many people have found that the intensity of the experience has brought their own spirituality in to sharper focus.

UCSF Medical Center:
Women and Children Without a Home

Hospitals are known for being locations which are regularly haunted. This is because the anguish experienced in the hospital setting is so intense, and so multiplied by the experience of pain had in the same location by so many others, that the likelihood of becoming trapped in the experience is much greater in hospitals than in any other average location. Most hospitals have their floors which workers know not to enter at certain times of the night or they have their tales about patients who have died in rooms but they then refused to leave.

The UCSF Medical Center is no exception to this experience. But the spirits who linger in this hospital are even more heartbreaking than those of many other hospitals. This is because our heartstrings are inevitably tugged by tales of wailing women and their dying children, and these are the spirits which seem to haunt this particular location.

The intensive care nursery and the pediatrics ward are the two spots in this hospital where the most hauntings have been reported (S.F. Heart, 2006). In the intensive care nursery, there are two kinds of spirits which linger; women who have died in childbirth who are wandering around looking for the children they never held in their arms and the children who were placed in intensive care and failed to make it out alive. In the pediatrics ward, the cries are frequently coming from the spirits of older children who didn't understand the pain they were enduring during their early deaths and have remained around trying to solve the mystery in order to cross over to another world.

Some may see these stories with a skeptical eye. Such is the nature, both of things which we don't completely understand such as haunting in general and of things which are too heartbreaking for us to easily accept in to our realities. However, some people took these experiences quite seriously, because there is record in the history of this hospital of an exorcism being held on the eighth floor to stop the trouble after it had gotten so bad that it was disturbing both patients and hospital staff.

The Ghost of Christopher Columbus:
When The Fog Changes

Is it possible that Christopher Columbus has decided to spend some of his afterlife floating above the streets of San Francisco? It seems to be an improbable notion, considering that San Francisco wasn't developed until centuries after the famous explorer had come and gone. However, it also seems to be a possibility given that his spirit has been sensed or seen by people located all throughout the Bay Area at different times in the course of history.

Christopher Columbus was born in the middle of the fifteenth century in Genoa and so is of Italian ancestry, although he is most commonly associated with the country of Spain because of his numerous links to the people of the country (specifically King Ferdinand and Queen Isabella). He was just fourteen when he took off on his first sea voyage (Pickering, 2006). And of course it is well known that in 1492, he sailed the ocean blue and gained credit as first discovering the Americas.

Despite his associations with this discovery, Christopher Columbus never spent time in what would become the San Francisco Bay Area. This area was certainly too far north of the locations which he was exploring for it to be feasible for him to have traveled up to the region. But in spite of this, sightings of his spirit have occurred throughout San Francisco.

The city does justice to the explorer (as do plenty of other locations) with a street named after him. Additionally, there is a statue of Christopher Columbus which stands atop Telegraph Hill at the famous Coit Tower, overlooking the bay. Perhaps it is because of these tributes that Columbus appears to make an appearance in the city every now and then. Or maybe it is because the city of San Francisco is a place which is respectful of the kind of adventuresome spirit which Columbus must have had in order to become the man that he was.

San Francisco simply accepts that change happens. Societal trends and cultural movements seem to take place in the city with relative ease. Tragedies are turned into moments in time which mark the alteration of millions of lives. This type of open attitude combines with the old frontier history of the region to create a place which lets the pioneer feel right at home. And maybe this is why Columbus comes to visit. Or maybe it is the reason why people here are willing to easily attribute the movement of spirits in the skies to someone like Columbus, a man who took off to the seas to see what was out there, never knowing if he would return.

Interestingly, it is not on the water that Christopher Columbus is most frequently reported to be seen. Although there have been occasional reports of sightings of ghostly boats passing through the bay, there are no hints that these boats are old enough to be linked with the timeless explorer. Instead, reports of his spirit are much more vague. Locals and travelers alike have said that they simply feel the suggestion of him, as a presence in the area.

In one case, a woman is said to have been standing by the statue of Christopher Columbus up near Coit Tower, when she felt a strange presence flood through her. She looked out across the water and saw that the clouds in the sky were beginning to swirl in unusual and indescribable patterns. She turned to the friends who had made the trek up Telegraph Hill with her and said, "Look at the fog ... it's changing!"

As soon as the words were out of her mouth, the clouds above her swirled into a shape which looked like the face of a man. A young child who was with the group pointed at the shape and then pointed at the statue of Christopher Columbus and said, "Look, that man is in the clouds." Everyone in the party felt a chill run down their spines. Then the clouds shifted again and the moment passed. The woman reports that the feeling doesn't coincide with any beliefs she has about the afterlife, and that she has no idea in the world why there would be the ghost of Christopher Columbus floating anywhere around San Francisco, but she also reports that despite being incapable of explaining what happened that day, she's certain that her life was touched by the famous explorer.

Sutro Baths:
Lingering at the Oceanside

In the late nineteenth century, one million dollars was a lot of money. But it wasn't too much for Adolph Sutro, the man behind one of the most extravagant leisure locations in historic San Francisco. The year was 1896, the man was a former mayor of the city, and the location was the west coast of the city. The creation was the Sutro Baths, a magnificent public bathhouse.

Many people have heard the term bathhouse and know only vaguely what this means. At their most basic, the Sutro Baths were a public swimming pool. But this slight description belies a much grander reality. This swimming pool area actually consisted of seven different swimming pools which were designed in Greek style within glass walls overlooking the Pacific Ocean. Toys for swimmers included diving boards and slides as well as trapezes and swings. Ten thousand people could fit into the baths at any given time.

For those people who wanted a break from the luxury of swimming in glass-encased magic, the Sutro Baths were also designed to be a place of leisure in other ways. There were three different restaurants located there so that visitors could ease the pangs of hunger worked up during swimming exercise. There was also an amphitheater featuring live stage performances of all kinds. Art gallery exhibits dotted the walls. The place was grandiose to a degree not even matched in the city to this day.

However, the venture proved to be less than fruitful. Perhaps this was because too much money went into the building to make it reasonable to keep it in operation. Maybe it was because the place was not easy to reach, since San Francisco was not built up at the time and the area required railroad travel to be accessed. Or maybe the Sutro Baths were just a little ahead—or a little behind—their times.

Whatever the case, the location underwent a number of changes throughout the years. For a time, it was an ice skating rink. After that, the general area became home to Playland at the Beach, a magnificent amusement park which drew in crowds in droves until it closed in the early 1970s.

All of this history makes it a haven for lingering spirits. The setting is perfect for having such an experience as well. The ruins of the baths are there to this day, located beneath the newly operating Cliff House Restaurant, right on the edge of the Pacific Ocean. Just north of the Sutro Bath ruins, there are a series of cave tunnels which lead out to a precarious perch on the water. Waves crash violently against the rocks at the end of these tunnels. One misstep and you could easily find yourself cascading into lost waters below.

But, if you brave the waves and the windy weather which accompanies them, and head out to the end of the tunnel with a candle, you may find spirits welcoming your presence. It is said that if you light the candle and place it at the end of the tunnel, then retreat, you will see a figure come along, pick up the candle, and toss it in to the water (S.F. Heart, 2006). Maybe it's the saddened spirit of Adolph Sutro whose dream was realized and then crushed by reality. Maybe it is a figure from the past who enjoyed the baths enough to never leave. Or maybe it is more than one presence from different parts of the history of the area who find the blurring of time and the beauty of nature here too irresistible to leave behind. (Pay close attention to the signs in the area that indicate which sections of the caves are physically safe for exploration.)

Out in the Ocean:
Ghost at Sea

Picture the stormy seas of San Francisco Bay on a frightening night in 1948. The captain loses control of the boat in a storm which catches the whole crew off guard. Only moments before the storm struck, the group on board the ship had been partying and enjoying a good time. Drinking had been going on for hours and many members of the ship's guest list were more than a little tipsy. One man, in particular, was obscenely drunk. He couldn't have kept his balance in the best of situations, and he certainly couldn't keep his balance on wobbling legs on an unsturdy ship tossing about on reckless seas. He fell overboard and was never heard from again. Or was he?

Eight years later, another tragic boat accident took place in the same area. This time, it was not a storm which caused the chaos aboard the ship but rather a fire. The entire crew had to abandon the ship and two men, named Eric and Peter, were among those who managed to get stranded at sea. Stuck in a small boat, they thought for sure that they were going to die of starvation while waiting for someone to figure out where they were.

Then a man appeared in a boat of his own, interested in helping them out. Both men blinked in astonishment when the man reached into the water and pulled out a fish, which he easily snapped in half. The two men were certain that they were hallucinating, but they agreed aloud that they could not possibly be sharing the same hallucination. They greedily accepted the fish which gave them enough energy to communicate with the man who offered to take them, in his boat, to a small island.

The offer was in exchange for some assistance. The man gave them an address which he said belonged to his wife. At the address was said to be a shed in which there was a key to a safe deposit box which they should inform his wife to access. At the island, he left Eric and Peter, safe on land but not sure where they were. They could only hope desperately that the man, who appeared more than a little crazy, would get them some help. He did. Shortly after the man left, the coast guard found Eric and Peter, saying that a man in a rowboat had indicated their location.

Shocked by their circumstances, they decided to follow the man's instructions. When they showed up on the doorstep of the woman said to be the rower's wife, they stunned her. "My husband was thrown overboard in a storm eight years ago," she explained. The men must have been charming, because she allowed them to enter the shed, where indeed was hidden a key. Upon further examination, the key did belong to a safe deposit box which turned out to hold the secret stash of money of the man too drunk to stay on his feet eight years before.

Maybe it's just a myth. Maybe it's just a ghost story. But maybe it's not...

Part VI:
A Professional Opinion:
Experts on Ghosts in the Bay Area

With its openness to the experience of a range of different activities, San Francisco has become the home (or sometimes the home-away-from-home) for numerous professionals involved in the business of contact with the dead. Psychics, mediums, ghost hunters, and numerous other experts in the area live their lives in regular association with the spirit world.

Some of the biggest names in psychic history have homes or businesses in the San Francisco Bay Area. The rich history of hauntings in San Francisco provides them much fodder for both personal and professional exploration into the possibilities of the world with a realm slightly beyond the one in which most of us live. San Francisco operates with an attitude which is simply conducive to the proliferation and success of such professions.

Amateur ghost hunters also thrive in the San Francisco area. There are so many different places in San Francisco and the surrounding area that are said to be haunted that it is easy for the amateur who is interested in ghostly experiences to spend some of his or her free time tracking them down and trying to get a little bit of insight in to the world comprised of the less-than-living.

In addition to the individuals who are well-known in the area for their work with the world of ghosts, as well as to those individuals who are part of the underground network of amateur ghost hunters in the area, there are groups which bring people of all ghost interest levels together. There are tours of the ghost histories of the area and conferences addressing modern issues in the world of ghost professionals today.

San Francisco is a city which is home to the strange, to the otherworldly, to the less-than-known. And it is a city where you can suspend your disbelief and allow yourself to get a glimpse of the other possibilities around you which are not at first visible to the eye. Just take a look at those professionals who are living their lives in close association with the ghost history of the area and you will see that there is certainly more than one way to live a life in San Francisco. And maybe even more than one way to experience your own afterlife!

Nick Nocerino:
Crystal Skulls and Spirit Worlds

Nick Nocerino is a jack-of-all-trades kind of guy in terms of his Bay Area ghosts experience. Known by some as a psychic and by others as a performer of exorcisms, Nocerino's hand touched the lives of many of those who discovered spirits in their homes and places of business. One of the major activities for which he is known is his experience in photographing spirit movement. However, he is actually best known as an expert on crystal skulls (Carroll, 2006).

Crystal skulls were unearthed in various parts of Latin America and have been a source of mystery since their discovery. Said to be as old as 36,000 years, these artifacts (the shape of heads created by crystallization) are of unknown origin. Even the fact that they have defied the laws of time and lasted despite their fragile nature is of mysterious interst to the researchers who are curious about their roots, researchers like Nick Nocerino (Shapiro, 2007).

Nocerino is said to have first begun to experience life with the other world through a dream which he had as a young child (Carroll, 2006). It is not uncommon for those who are able to closely experience the world of spirits to begin to have access to this knowledge at a young age. In fact, children may be more susceptible to such experiences than are their adult counterparts. In any case, Nocerino knew from the time he was a wee babe that he was touched with the ability to experience connections with the ghost world (Carroll, 2006).

Nocerino spent his lifetime pursuing those connections. Much of his adult life was spent working on understanding the nature of crystal skulls, which are said to have unknown origins and to be related to the spirit world. In fact, he is the founder of The Society of Crystal Skulls, an organization which uses science-based research methods to learn more about the skulls and their relationship to the rest of human history (Carroll, 2006). However, this was not a singular pursuit of Nocerino's. Open-minded in that true San Francisco fashion, Nocerino was interested in exploring as many different facets of this part of life (or afterlife) as was possible. As such, his life touched many of the locations of San Francisco and the surrounding area which have been reported to be haunted.

Entering a haunted location, Nocerino would spend time identifying the history of the area and the sense of spirits hovering there. He would then take photographs through which he would reveal the presence, and sometimes the character or identity, of the spirit in the location. His photographs helped to determine who was haunting both the Montandon Townhouse and the San Francisco Art Institute.

Nick Nocerino used his life to allow others to have increased understanding of the world of the dead. No longer with us in physical form today, Nick Nocerino may still be out there somewhere, connecting the worlds of the living and the spirits in ways we have yet to discover.

Sylvia Browne:
The Most Famous Psychic to Touch San Francisco

Best known for her regular appearances on the Montel Williams show, Sylvia Browne is a psychic with a lifetime of experience in communicating with spirits. She discovered her talents in this area when she was a mere three months old, and has devoted her life to using these talents to assist others in finding peace with the spirits in their lives (Browne, 2006). Originally from Kansas City, Missouri, she has been called in to the various sites of San Francisco on numerous occasions to provide her expert opinion on the spirits said to be haunting these spots.

Browne is a multi-talented woman; psychic, medium, author, celebrity speaker, and church founder are just a few of the titles she has to her name. She founded her own church, Novus Spiritus, over twenty years ago and has been working spiritually with others through the church since that time. The church is a loving church which does not believe in negative associations with God, but rather believes in celebrating God's love. This loving spirit has been infused in all of the work that she does (Browne, 2006).

Perhaps it is for this reason that spirits apparently communicate with Sylvia Browne. And perhaps it is for this reason that she has been well-received as an educated expert with an ability to communicate with the dead. Whatever the reason, Sylvia Browne has certainly been well-received, and she has spent much time in the Bay Area, offering her services to those with a need to find out what is happening with the unsettled of the area.

Three of the locations that Sylvia Browne has been known to explore and comment upon are the Mansions Hotel, the Atherton Mansion, and the Haskell House. At the Mansions Hotel, she reported sensing multiple spirits, although she could not identify them. At the Atherton Mansion, she was able to identify four distinct spirits and to provide information as to who they were and why they remained in the area. At the Haskell House, she discovered that there was not only the spirit of Terry Broderick haunting the location (as others believed) but that there had once been a slave plantation on the property and that the ghosts of the African American slaves who died there were still lingering.

By providing this information, Sylvia Browne has helped to establish credibility for the ghost stories of the Bay Area. Furthermore, she has helped others find peace with the situation in their homes because increased understanding of the nature of the hauntings helps them to settle their minds somewhat. Sylvia Browne continues to be active in psychic pursuits today.

Antoinette May:
Writer Contributes to San Francisco Ghost Knowledge

Antoinette May has worked in close connection with Sylvia Browne on several projects, including acting as the co-author for Browne's biography, *Adventures of a Psychic*. She is both a medium and a writer, working regularly for the *San Francisco Chronicle* as well as for other area publications.

May has contributed greatly to the amount of knowledge about the ghost world which is available to people interested in ghosts in San Francisco. She has written articles for numerous different publications which have provided much of the information that forms the foundation of knowledge of the topic in this area. In addition, she has participated in séances with Sylvia Browne to assist in determining the nature of the spirits in particular locations.

May's assistance with the biography of Sylvia Browne is one of her greatest contributions to the literature available on the topic of ghosts in San Francisco. Her other great contribution in this area is her book, *Haunted Houses of California: A Ghostly Guide*. Although not specific to San Francisco, this book adds greatly to the body of work which helps to bridge the gap between the worlds of those who are experts in San Francisco ghosts and those who merely want to get a handle on what it is that the experts have figured out.

Jim Fassbinder:
Ghost Tour Leader

Jim Fassbinder is a man who is known by tourists and locals alike as "that guy who gives the ghost tours". This is because he is the founder of the San Francisco Ghost Hunt, a two-hour-long walk through the historical experience of ghosts in the city of San Francisco. He launched the ghost tour in 1998, and currently operates tours every day of the week throughout most of the year (and six days a week throughout the rest of the year).

Fassbinder himself began experiencing connections with the spirit world when he was young and has worked ever since to incorporate these experiences into his daily life (San Francisco Ghost Hunt, 2006). He is a member of the Paranormal Research Organization as well as several other professional ghost organizations in the Bay Area and at the national level (San Francisco Ghost Hunt, 2006). He has consulted as a ghost expert on several projects and for several publications. A significant number of the locations explored throughout this book, including California Street and the Atherton Mansion, are locations which are viewed and discussed during Fassbinder's nightly tour. The tour begins at the Queen Anne Hotel where guests of the tour get their first up-close-and-personal chance to experience the ghosts which are famous in the history of San Francisco.

Jim Fassbinder is known in the area not merely for the fact that he decided to give a tour of the area's ghost history. He is known in the area because he does this tour so well, connecting those people who merely have an inkling of interest in the topic of San Francisco ghosts with those people and places who know those ghosts intimately. His ability to make this connection extends to adults and children alike; Fassbinder puts on an entire show during his tours, complete with costumes and elaborate stories which are designed to make the history of ghosts in the area accessible to everyone.

Tommy Netzband:
Walking Tour and Ghost Society

Jim Fassbinder's tour is not the only one in San Francisco that gets attention from those locals and travelers who are interested in experiencing what ghosts have to offer to the Bay Area. Although Fassbinder's tour is the one which is most well-known across the nation, there is also the Haunted Haight Walking Tour which provides information about areas of the city untouched by Fassbinder.

The Haight is one of the most famous of San Francisco's neighborhoods. It is known for being the location of the hippie movement, standing out above all other locations of the time as a place where change happened. Today, it is a tourist attraction but it is also enjoyed by those who live in the area because it is a place which continues to accept change and to challenge some of the boundaries of what is socially acceptable.

What better place than this for ghosts to have some reason to spend time in an area? The Haight, rich with history of all kinds, is a likely home for haunted experiences. And so the Haunted Haight Tour explores those experiences. Like Fassbinder's tour, this one is approximately two hours long. Locations are pointed out, although they are not explored in depth because most of them are homes in which people are living today, apparently unaffected by the ghostly presences within.

The tour is led by Tommy Netzband, a licensed tour guide who has over a decade of experience in paranormal research in the area (Haunted Haight Walking Tour Home Page, 2006). The tour is designed to be primarily a fun adventure, but it can also be an educational one, offering information to amateur ghost hunters which allows greater access to understanding the history of haunted locations in the happening Bay Area.

The Haunted Haight Walking Tour is not the only endeavor of Netzband's which touches San Francisco and the lives led there. In 2005, Netzband founded the San Francisco Ghost Society. The mission of this organization is "to promote awareness of paranormal phenomenon in the city of San Francisco, and to become a local resource of help and information for its citizens". People who have experienced potential contact with ghosts in the San Francisco area or who are concerned about the ghost activity in their homes in the city can contact the San Francisco Ghost Society to request an investigation. Investigations are performed by professionals who are affiliated with the San Francisco Ghost Society and are kept private (unpublished) to respect the rights of those who are learning to cope with ghost contact today.

Part VII:
See the Spirits:
Doing San Francisco Ghost Hunting on Your Own

Perhaps you have always wanted to experience the tingling sensation of having a close brush with someone from "the other side". Or maybe you simply have an interest in exploring some of the historical locations which are rife with ghost history. Or perhaps you are interested in preparing a special vacation for loved ones who are coming to visit you in San Francisco—something completely out of the ordinary and you are thinking that a tour of the city's haunted locations is the way to go.

Whatever your motivation for seeking out the city's spirits, there are a number of ways which you can choose to prepare for your own ghost hunt. Many people opt to organize their tours by type of location, exploring only the haunted hotels of the city or visiting only the haunted houses. Others choose to organize their ghost hunt tours by neighborhood. The two well-known organized tours of the city (Jim Fassbinder's San Francisco Ghost Hunt and Tommy Netzband's Haunted Haight Walking Tour) are each concentrated in different sections of the city and many people find it easy to simplify the travel portion of their tour by organizing them in a similar manner, focusing their ghost-hunt on a section of the city which is of particular interest to them.

There are a few things which you should keep in mind when you are in the process of organizing your own ghost hunt. First, you should realize that even places which are likely to be haunted may not always have active spirits present. You should approach your ghost hunt with an open mind and a willingness to just learn what there is to learn from the experience, rather than having some set notion of what in particular you are expecting to see.

Second, you should be respectful of the people who currently live in and around the locations which you are making a part of your ghost hunt. Many of the homes which are said to be haunted are currently being resided in by people making their lives in the city today, and they may have no interest in being as bothered by the living as they sometimes are by the dead. For this reason, you should be sure to do your research ahead of time, finding out in advance about whether or not the places you seek to explore are occupied. If so, you should get information as to whether or not visits are allowed. There are some spots that you may need to see only from the outside, and you should be respectful when taking pictures, making sure not to photograph residents and people conducting business in the area in the event that they don't want to be photographed.

Finally, you should remember to have fun. Ghost hunting can be an intense experience, especially for someone with a skeptical heart who finds out that there are some things out there which challenge their skepticism. Make the experience an enjoyable one by involving loved ones or new friends who are interested in exploring this part of the world with you. Take appropriate pictures and carry a journal to document your experiences. You just never know what you might find when you let yourself go out there in search of something new. And even if there aren't any ghosts turning up on your planned trips, you just might find that you learn some new things about the city and about your self which make your ghost hunting treks worthwhile.

Before You Go Ghost Hunting:
The Emotional Preparation

It is important for all people who are interested in going ghost hunting to engage in some emotional preparation before making the effort to start their search. It is critical to have a support network behind you filled with people who will believe what you say about your experience and who will help you in dealing with any emotional repercussions which may come from the event. It is also important to have internal resources to help you to understand the experience and the changes that you might undergo as a result of the experience. Even in cases where the individual ghost hunter feels comfortable with the spirit world, what sometimes happens is that the individual feels emotionally affected in unanticipated ways. It is best to prepare accordingly in order to avoid any problems with the ghost hunt. With proper preparation, the ghost hunt can be a terrifically enjoyable experience for all involved!

Whether or not you encounter spirits during your ghost hunt, you may find that the experience of engaging in the hunt can bring up emotional issues for you. Sometimes this is a result of the fact that the places which you are opting to explore at a deeper level are places which are filled with rich histories that are sometimes dotted with anguish or even overflowing with pain. When you go to explore these locations, you allow yourself to become enmeshed in the histories which are held within their walls, and you may find that this affects you at an emotional level, despite all of your predictions that it may not do so.

In some cases, people are interested in exploring the ghost stories which are related to their own personal histories. They may seek to learn about the ghosts which are experienced by others who have the same cultural background as themselves. Or they may go searching for an experience of ghost presence in the homes and places of business of their own and the people in their families. These experiences can bring up emotional trauma connected to the personal history of the ghost hunter.

Despite these risks, ghost hunting can be a terrifically fun experience and should not be avoided merely for fear of experiencing these negative effects. By properly preparing at the emotional level, it should be possible to gain insight into the areas of ghost hunting which you wish to explore without wreaking havoc on your own emotional life.

First and foremost, it is important that you prepare yourself with an in-depth look at your knowledge of yourself and what you can handle. If, for instance, you are aware of the fact that the areas in which you will be doing your ghost hunting are locations that might be of emotional significance to you, you should consider doing some work at the emotional level to understand your feelings about the experience before you embark on your adventures. Writing your thoughts down in a journal, talking your fears over with a close friend, or even consulting a professional who is capable of assisting you in dealing with the emotional effects of your journey are all methods which you might consider during this stage of emotionally preparing to engage in ghost hunting.

It is also important that you surround yourself with a network of people who are willing to support what you are doing. Consider, for example, the case of the man who has decided to go ghost hunting one weekend just to see what is out there. He doesn't even especially believe that ghosts necessarily exist, and he is fairly certain that he won't find anything, but he thinks that it might be fun to go exploring anyway. He picks his locations and he tells his wife about his plans. She is less than supportive but since he is kind of laughing and rolling his eyes about himself, she humors him and off he goes. When he returns, he is visibly shaken. He looks ... well, he looks like he has just seen a ghost.

The man does not know where to put this is in his schema of thought. He feels like his whole perspective on the world around him has become destabilized. And the real problem is that his wife, along with everyone else in his life, is living in disbelief of his experience. Perhaps she mocks him. Or perhaps she simply makes it known that she doesn't think that what he saw was real and that she doesn't want to hear any more about it. In either case, the man is not able to discuss his experience, so he stuffs it back inside of himself. In the best case scenario, he never goes any further in to exploring the world of ghosts. In a worse case, he becomes emotionally confused and frustrated, feeling like he is at a loss with nowhere to turn.

Of course, this is not going to be the case for everyone who goes ghost hunting. In many instances, the individual will go out, have some fun experiences and maybe pick up a story or two to tell around the dinner table at the holidays. But you simply never know what is going to happen when you go out to experience the greater world around you. As a result, it is important that you have people in your life who are able to help you cope with the unexpected if the experience is one which comes up for you.

If you find that you do not already have such an established network of emotional support in your life, you should seek out others who are like-minded in their ghost hunting interests with whom you can engage in ongoing discussion about the topic. This is a great idea anyway, because it can terrifically enhance your experience of the ghost hunting endeavor. Because of the great interest in and acceptance of ghostly activity in San Francisco, it is generally not difficult to find someone (or a group of people) with whom you can have such discussions. The available ghost hunt tours and ghost investigation groups in the area are one place to start. Or you can post on a website such as Craigslist (www.craigslist.org) to find people who have had experiences with ghosts or ghost hunting.

Creating this network of people who support you along with preparing yourself with knowledge of your own emotional status are the best methods of making sure that you are ready to go ghost hunting. All other preparation will be secondary to the emotional work that you can do to make the experience one which is full and complete and which offers all that you can possibly wish to get out of it to you in a safe manner.

Before You Go Ghost Hunting:
The Physical Preparation

Once you have laid down the emotional ground work to prepare you for going on your San Francisco Ghost Hunt, you will find that you have done most of what you need to do to get started. Everything after that is just secondary. However, you will want to do a little bit of physical preparation before you head out to enjoy your ghost hunt experience.

First of all, you will want to complete research on ghosts in the area which you are interested in studying. This will help prepare you as to what you might want to look for during your ghost hunt. Additionally, it will give you the background information which makes up the history of the area and provides you with the setting of any stories which you might discover for yourself on your trek. This research will also help you in narrowing down the locations which you are interested in exploring for your own ghost hunt, if you have not already done so.

Many people who have enjoyed ghost hunting in San Francisco have organized their hunts based on the neighborhoods of San Francisco. The city is one which is designed specifically by neighborhood, with each small segment of the area having an entirely different feel (and a mostly different history) from the rest of the city. More than almost any other city in the world, San Francisco is a place where you can travel just a few blocks in either direction from the location in which you are situated and be able to find yourself almost magically transported to what feels like a different world.

For example, from Chinatown it is possible to quickly walk to North Beach, Fisherman's Wharf, Telegraph Hill, the Financial District, the Tenderloin, Nob Hill and the SoMA area. This ability to experience different types of locations within such close geographic quarters creates the perfect setting for the merging of cultures and lives which helps to make San Francisco the type of place where spirits may wish to linger. By organizing a ghost hunt around different neighborhoods, you can truly experience each neighborhood in greater depth. Also, if you are planning to explore a number of different haunted locations during your ghost hunt, you may find that organizing your ghost hunting plans by neighborhood facilitates the process of moving smoothly from one location to another.

In addition to doing your background research, there may be some materials which you want to take along with you to help you to enjoy the ghost hunt experience to the fullest degree. No special tools are actually necessary for a San Francisco ghost hunt. As long as you have determined what the location is that you want to explore and checked out the logistics to make sure that the location is indeed a place which you are free to visit (a hotel open to the public as opposed to a private residence, for example), then you can go and indulge in the ghost hunt experience without additional accoutrements.

However, if you wish to document the experience or if you wish to more completely search for ghosts which may be located in the area of your exploration, there are certain tools which are recommended by experts in ghost hunting which might be right for the amateur ghost hunter. These tools may include cameras and/or video cameras, audio recording devices, night vision goggles, magnifying glasses and thermometers (Dwyer, 2005, p. 25 — 28).

Ghost hunters who are interested in attempting to capture their ghost hunting experience on camera have a few decisions to make. First, what needs to be determined is whether the desire is to photograph the ghost hunting experience as a whole or simply to try and catch images of ghosts on film. Secondly, the decision needs to be made as to whether still photographs or video camera work is the more preferred option of documentation.

Ghost hunters who wish to use photography to document their entire ghost hunt experience, for the purposes of a personal photo album or web page perhaps, will likely find that the standard digital camera which they already have in their possession is sufficient. This type of camera should be able to take decent pictures of the exterior and interior of any buildings or sites which are visited. However, ghost hunters who hope to capture actual images of ghosts on film will find that other camera equipment may be more useful to their project.

Experts in the field who have had successful photo documentation of ghosts generally recommend that a film camera be used rather than a digital camera. It is suggested that some experience be gained in the use of film which is sensitive to light and will allow for low-level light photographs to be taken without additional lighting being necessary (Dwyer, 2005, p. 26). Film which is above 800 ASA is what is most commonly recommended (Dwyer, 2005, p. 26). However, it is possible to document your ghost experiences using varying film, different types of cameras (including digital and Polaroid cameras) and adding the use of tripods and other equipment to enhance your photographic ability. Ghost hunters who become serious about the activity may wish to consider these options, but those who are just getting started may not want to invest the money up front.

Likewise, if you already own a video camera which can be used to document your experience, you may want to take it along. However, if you don't own one and are just getting started in your ghost hunting, you may want to hold off before making the investment. Different video recorders will offer a variety of options including timers, auto-focus options, and angle variation which can all make a difference in the quality of the video which you produce (Dwyer, 2005, p. 27).

In addition to video recording equipment, some ghost hunters take audio recording equipment with them. Tape recorders which are equipped to cut out background noise and enhance foreground sounds are frequently used by people who enjoy ghost hunting (Dwyer, 2005, p. 27). Sound-activated recorders and remote-location microphones are options which will allow the ghost hunter to record activity without being present in the location (Dwyer, 2005, p. 27). These latter options are generally not needed by the amateur ghost hunter, as they are unlikely to be allowed or legal in the public spaces which the ghost hunter is accessing. However, in rare cases where the ghost hunter is able to gain permission for the use of such items, they can certainly enhance the ghost hunting experience.

Other than equipment which is used to document the experience, the new ghost hunter may want to be sure to carry two other types of equipment. The first type of equipment which may be wanted is the set of accessories which can enhance the ghost hunting experience. This can include everything from high-end night vision goggles for searching through haunted locations in the dark to simple thermometers designed to measure temperature changes when ghostly drafts are felt. The second type of equipment which is almost a necessity is safety-based equipment, including a cell phone and a first aid kit in the event that something goes awry during the ghost hunt experience—the ghost hunter needs to be prepared.

Doing your own ghost hunting in San Francisco is relatively easy. There is a plethora of information available to assist in the research portion of the preparation for ghost hunting. There are professionals and tours in the area to assist with getting to know and access certain areas in the city. There are people willing to provide the emotional support necessary to do ghost hunting for those individuals who do not already have a strong support system in place in their lives. And there are plenty of haunted locations. The ghost hunting experience should be enjoyable, so get yourself prepared and then get out there and enjoy!

Conclusion

Spirits may be found in homes, hotels, schools and famous landmark locations. They may be left wandering the streets or the seas. They may move from place to place or they may stay stuck in a single room. The possibilities are seemingly endless. Whether you believe in them or not, the fact remains that many people in the world feel that they have experienced their lives as touched by ghosts. San Francisco is a location in which the proportion of people who feel this way seems to be higher than in many other spots.

While I knew that this was true before I began my research for this book, that research led me to an ever-greater understanding of the many different ways in which people here live their lives, ways which frequently include an acceptance of the possibility that we here on earth today may simply not know everything that there is to know about the world around us. With zero first-hand knowledge of ghost activity and nothing but a strong interest in the topic motivating me to learn more about it, I approached the writing of this book with an open mind but probably a skeptical heart.

What I was reminded of as I explored this world around me, was that an open mind can lead you to discover things about yourself and about others which you otherwise would not have known. As I got further in to my research, I found myself regularly sharing my findings with others in my life. And what I discovered was that nearly all of them had experienced some sort of brush with a world that they could not even begin to explain.

I found these stories happening in some of the most unexpected places. For example, I walked in to my personal trainer's gym one day and made a comment about the flickering light, only to discover that she was having unsettling experiences with ghost activity at home which she feared might have followed her to work. It took her a few days to open up about her experiences, but my openness to the topic allowed her to eventually feel comfortable enough to express her concerns over activity in her San Francisco home which she had previously thought was unthinkable.

Similarly, I went on a first date in which I ended up at a bookstore and found myself looking for new research material to complete this book. Used bookstores sometimes have that ghostly feeling about them anyway, because books have often lived a dozen lives, traveling from home to home before ending up on the shelves of the store. Standing in those aisles, looking for information about ghosts in the area, I asked my date about his beliefs in the world of ghosts. Although he prefaced his story with, "I'm not sure that I really believe this", he went on to tell me about the home that he had lived in as a child and how it had been haunted by a spirit which may or may not have been exorcised away.

The stories were abundant, and I discovered that the more I listened, the more that I learned. Like the man from that date, most people offered their stories with a sort of disclaimer—either they didn't believe in ghosts or they figured that there was some other explanation for what they were about to say, but ... and then they would continue with a story which seemed to have no other easy explanation. What I learned was that the topic is still a little bit taboo, but people certainly have a wealth of interesting stories about it stored within their brains and their family histories.

I learned that it is possible to suspend disbelief and simply be willing to find out what possibilities might exist around us. We don't have to believe wholeheartedly in every ghost story that we hear. But even those we don't believe in can be appreciated for what they are. Sometimes, that is merely a tale which entertains us. Other times, it is a story which gives us pause for thought. And in still other cases, it is the opportunity to get a new look at the history of an area which is filled with interesting tidbits of historical experience.

San Francisco is an endlessly interesting city, filled with eccentric people who lead creative and vibrant lives. It is no wonder that people who have lived there would want to remain there in their deaths. And it is no wonder that people who did not have the luxury of living there for long periods during their waking lives may want to experience the rest of their years in the midst of this welcoming city.

Today, tourists can learn about the history of the area, as well as the hauntings, through tours which are provided throughout the year. Currently, the city is home to two different walking tours specific to locating and exploring the ghosts of the city. In addition, there is a vampire tour which looks at the history of this unique counterpart to the ghost as it has been said to be experienced in the Bay Area. And if you opt not to take a tour, but sit quietly for long enough, you just might find that history is walking a little bit closer than you might have thought.

The following section is provided by the Chester County Paranormal Research Society in Pennsylvania and appears in training materials for new investigators.

Please visit www.ChesterCountyprs.com for more information.

Glossary

Air Probe Thermometer
A thermometer with an external probe that is capable of taking instant measurements of the air temperature.

Anomalous field
A field that can not be explained or ruled out by various possibilities, that can be a representation of spirit or paranormal energy present.

Apparition
A transparent form of a human or animal, a spirit.

Artificial field
A field that is caused by electrical outlets, appliances, etc.

Aural Enhancer
A listening device that enhances or amplifies audio signals. i.e., Orbitor Bionic Ear.

Automatic writing
The act of a spirit guiding a human agent in writing a message that is brought through by the spirit.

Base readings
The readings taken at the start of an investigation and are used as a means of comparing other readings taken later during the course of the investigation.

Demonic Haunting
A haunting that is caused by an inhuman or subhuman energy or spirit.

Dowsing Rods
A pair of L-shaped rods or a single Y-shaped rod, used to detect the presence of what the person using them is trying to find.

Electro-static generator
A device that electrically charges the air often used in paranormal investigations/research as a means to contribute to the materialization of paranormal or spiritual energy.

ELF
Extremely Low Frequency.

ELF Meter/EMF Meter
A device that measures electric and magnetic fields.

EMF
Electro Magnetic Field.

EVP
Electronic Voice Phenomena.

False positive
Something that is being interpreted as paranormal within a picture or video and is, in fact, a natural occurrence or defect of the equipment used.

Gamera
A 35mm film camera connected with a motion detector that is housed in a weather proof container and takes a picture when movement is detected. Made by Silver Creek Industries.

Geiger Counter
A device that measures gamma and x-ray radiation.

Infra Red
An invisible band of radiation at the lower end of the visible light spectrum. With wavelengths from 750 nm to 1 mm, infrared starts at the end of the microwave spectrum and ends at the beginning of visible light. Infrared transmission typically requires an unobstructed line of sight between transmitter and receiver. Widely used in most audio and video remote controls, infrared transmission is also used for wireless connections between computer devices and a variety of detectors.

Intelligent haunting
A haunting of a spirit or other entity that has the ability to interact with the living and do things that can make its presence known.

Milli-gauss
Unit of measurement, measures in 1000th of a gauss and is named for the famous German mathematician, Karl Gauss.

Orbs
Anomalous spherical shapes that appear on video and still photography.

Pendulum
A pointed item that is hung on the end of a string or chain and is used as a means of contacting spirits. An individual will hold the item and let it hang from the finger tips. The individual will ask questions aloud and the pendulum answers by moving.

Poltergeist haunting
A haunting that has two sides, but same kinds of activity in common. Violent outbursts of activity with doors and windows slamming shut, items being thrown across a room and things being knocked off of surfaces. Poltergeist hauntings are usually focused around a specific individual who resides or works at the location of the activity reported, and, in some cases, when the person is not present at the location, activity does not occur. A poltergeist haunting may be the cause of a human agent or spirit/energy that may be present at the location.

Portal
An opening in the realm of the paranormal that is a gateway between one dimension and the next. A passageway for spirits to come and go through. See also Vortex.

Residual haunting
A haunting that is an imprint of an event or person that plays itself out like a loop until the energy that causes it has burned itself out.

Scrying
The act of eliciting information with the use of a pendulum from spirits.

Table Tipping
A form of spirit communication, the act of a table being used as a form of contact. Individuals will sit around a table and lightly place there fingertips on the edge of the table and elicit contact with a spirit. The Spirit will respond by "tipping" or moving the table.

Talking Boards
A board used as a means of communicating with a spirit. Also known as a Quija Board.

Vortex
A place or situation regarded as drawing into its center all that surrounds it.

White Noise
A random noise signal that has the same sound energy level at all frequencies.

EQUIPMENT EXPLANATIONS

In this section, the Chester County Paranormal Research Society looks at the application and benefits of equipment used on investigations with greater detail. The equipment used for an investigation plays a vital role in the ability to collect objective evidence and helps to determine what is and is not paranormal activity. But a key point to be made here is: the investigator is the most important tool on any investigation. With that said, let us now take a look at the main pieces of equipment used during an investigation...

The Geiger Counter

The Geiger counter is device that measures radiation. A "Geiger counter" usually contains a metal tube with a thin metal wire along its middle. The space in between them is sealed off and filled with a suitable gas and with the wire at about +1000 volts relative to the tube. An ion or electron penetrating the tube (or an electron knocked out of the wall by X-rays or gamma rays) tears electrons off atoms in the gas. Because of the high positive voltage of the central wire, those electrons are then attracted to it. They gain energy that collide with atoms and release more electrons, until the process snowballs into an "avalanche", producing an easily detectable pulse of current. With a suitable filling gas, the flow of electricity stops by itself, or else the electrical circuitry can help stop it. The instrument was called a "counter" because every particle passing it produced an identical pulse, allowing particles to be counted, usually electronically. But it did not tell anything about their identity or energy, except that they must have sufficient energy to penetrate the walls of the counter. The Geiger counter is used in paranormal research to measure the background radiation at a location. The working theory in this field is that paranormal activity can effect the background radiation. In some cases, it will increase the radiation levels and in other cases it will decrease the levels.

Digital and 35mm Film Cameras

The camera is an imperative piece of equipment that enabled us to gather objective evidence during a case. Some of the best evidence presented from cases of paranormal activity over the years has been because of photographs taken. If you own your own digital camera or 35mm film camera, you need to be fully aware of what the cameras abilities and limitations are. Digital cameras have been at the center of great debate in the field of paranormal research over the years. The earlier incarnations of digital cameras were full of inherent problems and notorious for creating "false positive" pictures. A "false positive" picture is a picture that has anomalous elements within the picture that are the result of a camera defect or other natural occurrence. There are many pictures scattered about the internet that claim to be of true paranormal activity, but in fact they are "false positives." Orbs, defined as anomalous paranormal energy that can show up as balls of light or streaks in still photography or video, are the most controversial pictures of paranormal energy in the field. There are so many theories (good and bad) about the origin of orbs and what they are. Every picture in the CCPRS collection that has an orb—or orbs—are not presented in a way that state that they are absolutely paranormal of nature. I have yet to capture an orb photo that made me feel certain that in fact it is of a paranormal nature. If you use your own camera, understand that your camera is vital. I encourage all members who own their own cameras to do research on the make and model of the camera and see what other consumers are saying about them. Does the manufacturer give any info regarding possible defects or design flaws with that particular model? Understanding your camera will help to rule out the possibility of interpreting a "false positive" for an authentic picture of paranormal activity.

Video Cameras

The video camera is also a fundamental tool in the investigation as another way for collecting objective evidence that can support the proof of paranormal activity. The video camera can be used in various ways during the investigation. It can be set on a tripod and left in a location where paranormal activity has been reported. It can also be used as a hand-held camera and the investigator will take it with them during their walk through investigation as a means of documenting to hopefully capture anomalous activity on tape. Infra-Red technology has become a feature on most consumer level video cameras and depending on the manufacturer can be called "night shot" or "night alive." What this technology does is allow us to use the camera in zero light. Most cameras with this feature will add a green tint or haze to the camera when it is being used in this mode. A video camera with this ability holds great appeal to the paranormal investigator.

EMF/ELF Meters

EMF=Electro Magnetic Frequency   ELF=Extremely Low Frequency

What is an EMF/ELF meter? Good question. The EMF/ELF meter is a meter that measures Electric and Magnetic fields in an AC or DC current field. It measures in a unit of measurement called "milli-gauss," named for the famous German mathematician, Karl Gauss. Most meters will measure in a range of 1-5 or 1-10 milli-gauss. The reason that EMF meters are used in paranormal research is because of the theory that a spirit or paranormal energy can add to the energy field when it is materializing or is present in a location. The theory says that, typically, an energy that measures between 3-7 milli-gauss may be of a paranormal origin. This doesn't mean that an artificial field can't also measure within this range. That is why we take base readings and make maps notating where artificial fields occur. The artificial fields are a direct result of electricity, i.e. wiring, appliances, light switches, electrical outlets, circuit breakers, high voltage power lines, sub-stations, etc. The Earth emits a naturally occurring magnetic field all around us and has an effect on paranormal activity. Geo-magnetic storm activity can also have a great influence on paranormal activity. For more information on this kind of phenomena visit: www.noaa.sec.com. There are many different types of EMF meters; and each one, although it measures with the same unit of measurement, may react differently. An EMF meter can range from anywhere to $12.00 to $1,000.00 or more depending on the quality and features that it has. Most meters are measuring the AC (alternating current, the type of fields created by man-made electricity) fields and some can measure DC (direct current-naturally occurring fields, batteries also fall into the category of DC) fields. The benefit of having a meter that can measure DC fields is that they will automatically filter out the artificial fields created by AC fields and can pick up more naturally occurring electro magnetic fields. Some of the higher-tech EMF meters are so sensitive that they can pick up the fields generated by living beings. The EMF meter was originally designed to measure the earth's magnetic fields and also to measure the fields created by electrical an artificial means. There have been various studies over the years about the long term effects of individuals living in or near high fields. There has been much controversy as to whether or not long term exposure to high fields can lead to cancer. It has been proven though that no matter what, long term exposure to high fields can be harmful to your health. The ability to locate these high fields within a private residence or business is vital to the investigation. We may offer suggestions to the client as to possible solutions for dealing with high fields. The wiring in a home or business can greatly affect the possibility of high fields. If the wiring is old and/or not shielded correctly, it can emit high fields that may affect the ability to correctly notate any anomalous fields that may be present.

Audio Recording Equipment

Audio recording equipment is used for conducting EVP (Electronic Voice Phenomena) research and experiments. What is an EVP? An EVP is a phenomenon where paranormal voices or sounds can be captured with audio recording devices. The theory is that the activity will imprint directly onto the device or tape, but has not been proven to be an absolute fact. The use of an external microphone is essential when conducting EVP experiments with analog recording equipment. The internal microphone on an analog tape recorder can pick up the background noise of the working parts within the tape recorder and can taint the evidence as a whole. Most digital recorders are quiet enough to use the internal microphone, but as a general rule of thumb, we do not use them. An external microphone will be used always. Another theory about EVP research is that an authentic EVP will happen within the range 250-400hz. This is a lower frequency range and isn't easily heard by the human ear, and the human voice does not emit in this range. EVP is rarely heard at the moment it happens—it is usually revealed during the playback and analysis portion of the investigation.

Thermometers

The use of a thermometer in an investigation goes without saying. This is how we monitor the temperature changes during the course of an investigation. CCPRS is currently using Digital thermometers with remote sensors as a way to set up a perimeter and to notate any changes in a stationary location of an investigation. The Air-probe thermometer can take "real time" readings that are instantly accurate. This is the more appropriate thermometer for measuring air temperature and "cold spots" that may be caused by the presence of paranormal phenomena. The IR Non-contact thermometer is the most misused thermometer in the field of paranormal research. CCPRS does not own or use IR Non-contact thermometers for this reason. The IR (infra-red) Non-contact thermometer is meant for measuring surface temperatures from a remote location. It shoots an infrared beam out to an object and bounces to the unit and gives the temperature reading. I have seen, first hand, investigators using this thermometer as a way to measure air temperature. NO, this is not correct! Enough said. In an email conversation that I have had with Grant Wilson from TAPS, he has said that, "Any change in temperature that can't be measured with your hand is not worth notating…"

Bibliography

Albert, Janice (2006). *Gertrude Atherton (1857 — 1948).* California Association of Teachers of English (CATE) web page. Retrieved August 2, 2006 from http://www.cateweb.org/ CA_Authors/Atherton.htm.

Browne, Sylvia (2006). *Sylvia Browne: Psychic and Spiritual Teacher.* The Official Sylvia Browne Website. Retrieved December 1, 2006 from http://www.sylvia.org/home/index.cfm.

Cameron, Donaldina (1939). *Chinese Home Moves.* The San Francisco News. The Virtual Museum of the City of San Francisco. Retrieved December 5, 2006 from http://www. sfmuseum.org/1906/ew15.html.

Carroll, Robert Todd (2006). *Crystal Skull.* The Skeptic's Dictionary. Retrieved December 1, 2006 from http://skepdic.com/crystalskull.html.

Chinese Christian Schools (2006). *Chinese Christian Schools: Transforming Lives for the Glory of God.* Retrieved September 18, 2006 from http://www.ccs-rams.org.

Crawford, Tom (2002). *The Queen Anne Hotel: San Francisco, California.* Ghost Source: Your Portal To The Paranormal. Retrieved January 1, 2007 from http://www.ghostsource. com/location_oct2002.html.

Collins, Tess (2003). *How Theater Managers Manage.* Retrieved January 1, 2007 from http:// home.pacbell.net/tessala/howmanage.html.

Crissy Field Center (2006). *Crissy Field Web Page.* Retrieved December 4, 2006 from htpp://www. crissyfield.org.

Donat, Hank (2001). *Notorious San Francisco: Pat Montandon's Curse.* MisterSF.com: Heart of the City. Retrieved December 6, 2006 from http://www.mistersf.com/notorious/index/ html?intructers.htm.

Dwyer, Jeff. *Ghost Hunter's Guide to the San Francisco Bay Area.* Gretna, Louisiana: Pelican Publishing company, 2005.

Flood Building Web Page. *Flood Building History.* Retrieved November 5, 2006 from http://www. floodbuilding.com.

Foreman, Laura (1999). *Discovery Travel Adventure Haunted Holidays.* Excerpted at Travel Channel Feature: Mysterious Journeys. Retrieved November 7, 2006 from http://travel. discovery.com/convergence/hauntedtdravels/interactives/sanfrancisco/institute.html.

GAzis-SAx, Joel (1996). *The Murder And Afterlife Of Senator David Broderick: A Skeptical Appreciation of a Haunting.* Tales From Colma. Retrieved September 8, 2006 from http://www. notfrisco.com/colmatales.broderick.

Graf, Hilber (2006). *Ghost Hunting in Mother Lode Country*. Buy Books On The Web. Retrieved December 20, 2006 from http://www.buybooksontheweb.com/peek.asp?ISBN=0-7414-2963-2.

Hauck, Dennis William. *San Francisco's Most Haunted*. Haunted Places Directory. Retrieved July 28, 2006 from http://www.haunted-places.com/san_francisco_most_haunted.htm.

Haunted Bay Home Page. Retrieved July 30, 2006 from www.hauntedbay.com.

Haunted Haight Walking Tour Home Page. Retrieved September 15, 2006 fromhttp://hauntedhaight.com.

Hill, Toya Richards (2006). *Let The Healing Begin: San Francisco's Cameron House Confronts 40 Years of Sexual Abuse*. Presbyterian News Service. Worldwide Faith News. Retrieved December 6, 2006 from http://www.wfn.org/2006/06/msg00029.html.

Hotel Union Square Home Page. Retrieved December 30, 2006 from http://www.hotelunionsquare.com/html/dashiell-hammett.html.

Hotel Majestic Home Page. Retrieved July 15, 2006 from html://www.thehotelmajestic.com/history.html.

International Al Jolson Society (2006). *Al Jolson: The World's Greatest Entertainer.* Retrieved January 1, 2007 from http://www.jolson.org.

Jones, Michael (2000). *The 'Haunted Mansions Hotel Investigation'*. Retrieved December 14, 2006 from http://www.customvb.net/u/litd/_Unexplained/mansions/mansions.shtml.

Kirjasto (2006). *Lillian Hellman (1905 — 1984)*. Pegasos. Retrieved December 14, 2006 from http://www.kirjasto.sci.fi/.

May, Antoinette. *Is There a Spirit Here Tonight?* San Francisco Chronicle. October 31, 2004. Retrieved October 25, 2006 from http://www.sfgate.com/cgi-bin/article.cgi?file=.chronicle/archive/2004/10/31/PKGMK9GJ381.DTL.

May, Antoinette (2006). *Travel: The Ghosts Who Come To Dinner.* Sacramento Magazine. Retrieved December 24, 2006 from http://www.sacmag.com/media/Sacramento-Magazine/October-2006/Travel-The-Ghosts-Who-Come-to-Dinner/.

Merriman, C.D. (2005). *Gertrude Franklin Horn Atherton*. The Literature Network. Retrieved December 14, 2006 from http://www.online-literature.com/gertrude-atherton/.

Montandon, Pat (2001). *Pat Montandon: Author — Speaker.* Pat Montandon Home Page. Retrieved December 20, 2006 from http://www.patmontandom.com.

Morrison, Michael (2006). *To The Manner Born*. Shakespearean.com Web Page. Retrieved November 4, 2006 from http://wwwshakespearean.com/Biography.htm.

National Park Conservation Association (MPCA) (2006). *Revitalized Crissy Field Draws People, Wildlife: Renovation Restores Wetlands and History to Recreational Site*. Retrieved August 7, 2006 from http://www.npca.org/marine_and_coastal/wetlands/crissy_field.html.

National Register of Historic San Francisco (NRHSF). *Landmark 76000524: Whittier Mansion*. Retrieved October 4, 2006 from http://www.noehill.com/sf/landmarks/nat1976000524.asp.

Olmsted, Roger & Watkins, T.H. (1969). *Here Today, San Francisco's Architectural Heritage.* San Francisco: Chronicle Books. Online version retrieved from Vernacular Language North on December 4, 2006 from http://www.verlang.com/sfbay0004ref_19thc_016. html#2090_Jackson.

Pearson, David B. (2005). *Arbucklemania: The Roscoe "Fatty" Arbuckle Web Site.* Retrieved January 1, 2007 from http://silent-movies.com/Arbucklemania/home.html.

Pickering, Keith. *The Columbus Navigation Home Page.* Retrieved December 1, 2006 from http://www.columbusnavigation.com.

Richards, Rand. *Haunted San Francisco: Ghost Stories from the City's Past.* San Francisco, CA: Heritage House Publishers, 2004.

San Francisco Art Institute (SFAI) (2006). *San Francisco. Art. Institute.* Retrieved November 11, 2006 from http://www.sfai.edu.

San Francisco Ghost Hunt Home Page. Retrieved August 31, 2006 from http://www.sfghost-hunt.com.

S. F. Heart. *Haunted Places in San Francisco.* Retrieved October 1, 2006 from http://www.sfheart. com/Haunted_San_Francisco.html.

Shapiro, Joshua (2007). *Strange Artifacts: Crystal Skulls.* World-Myserties.com. Retrieved March 2, 2007 from http://www.world-mysteries.com.

Spataro, Margarita. *Haunted in San Francisco.* The Guardsman Online: City College of San Francisco. October/November 1999. Retrieved July 24, 2006 from http://www.ccsf.edu/ Events_Pubs/Guardsman/f991025/feat01.shtml.

StrangeUSA.com (2006). *Abandoned Army Hospital.* Retrieved October 4, 2006 from http://www. strangeusa.com/viewhunt.asp?haunted=949.

Styles, Margaret (2002). *Final Flight.* Presidio of San Francisco. National Park Service. Retrieved November 16, 2006 from http://www.nps.gov/archive/prsf/history/crissy/crisybio.htm.

Thomas, Vicki (2003). *Cameron, Donaldina (Mackenzie): Missionary, Social Worker and Youth Advocate.* Encyclopedia of San Francisco. Retrieved December 5, 2006 from http://www. sfhistoryencyclopedia.com/articles/c/cameronDonaldina.html.

Weirde, Dr. (2006). *The Haunted House on The Crookedest Street: The Montndon Townhouse.* Dr. Weirde's Guide To Mysterious San Francisco. Offbeat. Retrieved December 4, 2006 from http://www.sfgate.com/offbeat/pat.html.

Westin St. Francis Home Page (2006). *A Colorful Past: The Paris of the West.* Retrieved December 5, 2006 from http://www.westinstfrancis.com/default2.asp?sID=Hist.

Whitington, Mitchel (2001). *A Ghost in My Suitcase: A Guide To Haunted Travel In America.* Ghost In My Suitcase Web Page. Retrieved October 17, 2006 from http://www.ghostinmysuitcase. com/places/queenanne/index.htm.

Wikipedia (2006). *Loma Prieta Earthquake.* Retrieved December 4, 2006 from http://en.wikipedia. org/wiki/Loma_Prieta_earthquake#1989_World_Series.

Zellerbach, Merla (2001). *Pat Montandon: From Party Girl To Peacenik.* Nob Hill Gazette. Retrieved from Pat Montandon Website on December 6, 2006 from http://patmontandon. com/articles.htm.